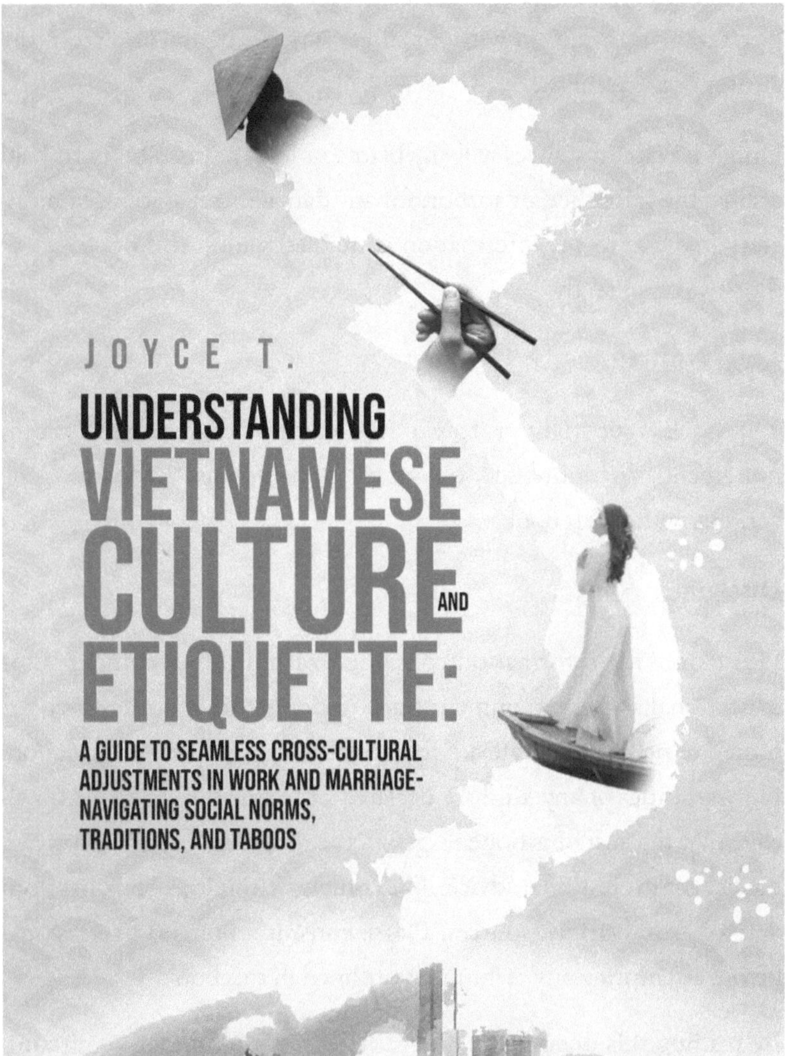

JOYCE T.

UNDERSTANDING VIETNAMESE CULTURE AND ETIQUETTE:

A GUIDE TO SEAMLESS CROSS-CULTURAL ADJUSTMENTS IN WORK AND MARRIAGE- NAVIGATING SOCIAL NORMS, TRADITIONS, AND TABOOS

© Copyright 2023 - **All rights reserved.**

The content contained within this book may not be reproduced, duplicated or transmitted without direct written permission from the author or the publisher.

Under no circumstances will any blame or legal responsibility be held against the publisher, or author, for any damages, reparation, or monetary loss due to the information contained within this book, either directly or indirectly.

<u>Legal Notice:</u>

This book is copyright protected. It is only for personal use. You cannot amend, distribute, sell, use, quote or paraphrase any part, or the content within this book,

<u>Disclaimer Notice:</u>

Please note the information contained within this document is for educational and entertainment purposes only. All effort has been executed to present accurate, up to date, reliable, complete information. No warranties of any kind are declared or implied. Readers acknowledge that the author is not engaged in the rendering of legal, financial, medical or professional advice. The content within this book has been derived from various sources. Please consult a licensed professional before attempting any techniques outlined in this book.

By reading this document, the reader agrees that under no circumstances is the author responsible for any losses, direct or indirect, that are incurred as a result of the use of the information contained within this document, including, but not limited to, errors, omissions, or inaccuracies.

CONTENTS

INTRODUCTION

Hello there! Welcome aboard. We're about to embark on a little adventure - a jaunt into the heartland of Vietnamese culture, if you will. But fear not; we're not going to get lost in translation or swamped in cultural conundrums.

Now, you might be wondering, "Why on earth do I need to understand Vietnamese etiquette?" Well, I'll tell you. Whether you're planning to travel, work, marry, or adopt in Vietnam or simply want to broaden your understanding of different cultures, getting the hang of the local customs can be the difference between a smooth ride and a bumpy detour.

This book will guide you through the mazes of etiquette, societal norms, and everyday life in Vietnam. It's designed to be your trusty companion, whether you're navigating the bustling streets of Hanoi, attending a traditional wedding, or trying to impress your Vietnamese in-laws with your impeccable manners.

I'll bet you've heard lots of things about Vietnam - its lively cities, lush landscapes, delectable pho, and vibrant history. But Vietnam is so much more than that. It's a country of unspoken rules, subtle gestures, and deep-rooted traditions. It's a place where a nod can speak volumes and where the gift of fruit can be a heartfelt token of respect.

And who am I to guide you through this cultural labyrinth? I'm Vietnamese myself, and I'm a writer with a passion for breaking down cultural barriers. I've spent years immersing myself in my own culture, and now, I'm ready to share my insights and experiences with you.

So, buckle up! Together, we're about to explore the fascinating and sometimes complex nature of Vietnamese culture. Let's get started, shall we?

CHAPTER ONE

VIETNAM AND ITS PEOPLE

At the heart of this vibrant culture lies three key aspects: strong family ties, deep reverence for ancestors, and the profound influence of Buddhism and Confucianism. In this chapter, we will cover each in detail, starting with family ties.

1.1 Vietnamese Society - The Unbreakable Family Ties

Vietnamese value family above everything; for them, family is not just a social unit; it's a strong support network that influences every aspect of their lives.

These familial bonds are not limited to the nuclear family. The connection extends to a wide network of relatives, including aunts, uncles, cousins, and even distant relatives. Similar to a single thread, a Vietnamese family on its own might seem insignificant. However, when these families come together, they create a powerful and supportive network, much like a strong, woven fabric.

Every family member has a clear role, and they strive to fulfill it to the best of their ability. So, if you're planning to be part of a Vietnamese family, remember, you're not just marrying a person but an entire family.

The Role of Ancestors in Daily Life

The Vietnamese never forget their roots. Ancestors play a significant role in Vietnamese culture. They are not merely a part of history but are considered an integral part of the family, even in their afterlife.

Ancestor worship is a common practice across Vietnam. Many homes have an altar dedicated to their ancestors, where daily offerings are made and prayers are said. It's like having a daily call with your grandparents, keeping them updated on your life, and seeking their blessings.

Ancestor worship is not limited to the home. They are remembered and honored in significant life events, be it a wedding, a birth, or even before starting a new business. It's as if the ancestors are always there, watching over their families, guiding them, and sharing in their joys and sorrows.

The Influence of Buddhism and Confucianism

If the family forms the roots of Vietnamese society, Buddhism and Confucianism are the sunshine and rain nurturing this tree. These philosophies deeply influence the Vietnamese way of life, shaping their attitudes, beliefs, and behaviors.

Buddhism's teachings of peace, compassion, and detachment play a significant role in Vietnamese society. It's not just seen as a religion but more as a way of life, a guide to leading a peaceful and fulfilling life.

You can see Buddhism's influence in the Vietnamese's calm demeanor, resilience in the face of adversity, and contentment with life's simple pleasures. They believe in living in the moment, cherishing the now rather than worrying about the past or the future.

On the other hand, Confucianism, with its emphasis on order, hierarchy, and harmony, molds the social dynamics in Vietnam. It guides interpersonal relationships and social conduct, promoting respect for elders and authority, family loyalty, and relationship harmony.

Confucian values are deeply embedded in Vietnamese society. You can see it in the respect students show to their teachers, the deference employees show to their bosses, and the reverence children have for their parents.

So, if you ever find yourself in a Vietnamese gathering, remember to greet the oldest person first. It's a small gesture but a significant reflection of your understanding and respect for Vietnamese culture.

Like a well-tended tree, Vietnamese culture stands tall and proud, with its roots firmly grounded in strong family ties, deep respect for ancestors, and the enriching teachings of Buddhism and Confucianism. As we delve deeper into this fascinating culture, keep these foundational aspects in mind. They will help you understand the nuances of Vietnamese etiquette and navigate your interactions with the locals more effectively.

But remember, every tree is unique, just like every individual. So, while these cultural insights provide a broad understanding, always respect individual differences and personal beliefs. After all, isn't that what cultural understanding is all about?

1.2 Vietnamese History in a Nutshell

You know how a gust of wind can sway a tree, but its roots keep it grounded? The history of Vietnam is a bit like that. The country has faced numerous external influences and tumultuous periods, which have swayed its course but have not uprooted its rich cultural heritage. Let's take a brisk walk down memory lane and explore the key historical periods that have shaped modern-day Vietnam.

The Era of Chinese Domination

When the Chinese Han Dynasty annexed Vietnam in 111 BC, the country found itself under a different set of rules, norms, and ideologies. For the next thousand years, Vietnam was under Chinese rule, and this period was marked by continuous efforts by the Vietnamese people to retain their distinct cultural identity while navigating through the imposed Chinese administration, language, and customs.

The Chinese introduced their legal codes, bureaucracy, and Confucian educational system. They also brought advancements in agriculture, pottery, and metallurgy. But the Vietnamese, holding on to their resolve, managed to preserve their indigenous culture. They held onto their language, folklore, and unique way of life.

Finally, in 938 AD, after many revolts and uprisings, Vietnam regained its independence at the Battle of Bach Dang River, finally breaking free from the Chinese.

The French Colonial Period

Fast forward a few centuries to the mid-19th century. Vietnam now had to face another storm - French colonization. The French rule, which lasted from the 1850s to 1954, brought significant changes to Vietnamese society, economy, and culture.

Under French rule, Vietnam underwent urbanization, with the establishment of infrastructure, public works, and new industries. The French introduced their language, education system, and Roman Catholic religion. They also brought their cuisine, resulting in the unique fusion of flavors we see in Vietnamese food today.

However, the French colonizers exploited the country's resources. They imposed harsh policies, leading to widespread dissatisfaction and resistance among the Vietnamese people. During this period, a strong sense of nationalism emerged, leading to organized efforts to reclaim independence.

The Vietnam War and Its Aftermath

The next big wave to hit Vietnam was the Vietnam War, a tumultuous period that left deep scars on the country and its people. The war, which lasted from 1954 to 1975, was a struggle between the communist forces of North Vietnam, backed by China and the Soviet Union, and the non-communist forces of South Vietnam, supported by the United States.

The Vietnam War was a period of intense conflict, devastating bombings, and widespread anti-war protests worldwide. The war ended in 1975 with the fall of Saigon, marking the reunification of North and South Vietnam under communist rule.

The war's aftermath was a challenging period for Vietnam, with economic hardships, social upheaval, and the daunting task of rebuilding a war-torn country. However, like a tree sprouting new leaves after a harsh winter, Vietnam embarked on a process of renewal and recovery.

In the late 1980s, Vietnam introduced economic reforms known as the Đổi Mới, shifting from a centrally planned economy to a socialist-oriented market economy. These reforms led to rapid economic growth, reduced poverty rates, and improved living standards.

Today, Vietnam stands as a testament to resilience and recovery. It's a rapidly developing country, embracing modernization and globalization yet firmly rooted in its rich cultural heritage and historical legacy. As we continue to explore Vietnamese culture in the following chapters, remember that this resilient spirit, this ability to endure, adapt, and grow, is an integral part of the Vietnamese ethos. It's what makes Vietnam the fascinating, multifaceted country it is today.

1.3 Understanding the Vietnamese Way of Thinking

The Concept of "Face" in Vietnamese Culture

A significant concept in Vietnamese society is the notion of "face" or "saving face." You might be imagining it as some sort of skincare ritual. However, it's more about protecting one's reputation and social standing. In a nutshell, "face" is all about maintaining dignity and respect in public.

The concept of "face" influences various aspects of Vietnamese society, from business transactions to social interactions. It encompasses a delicate balance of giving face (showing respect), saving face (avoiding embarrassment), and losing face (damaging one's reputation).

For instance, public criticism or confrontation is generally avoided as it could cause someone to "lose face." Similarly, showing respect to elders and superiors is a way of "giving face." So, if you're in a Vietnamese social setting, remember, it's not just about your face but also about saving and giving "face" to others.

The Importance of Harmony and Balance

The Vietnamese way of thinking has a profound sense of balance. It's like the yin and yang, each aspect of life complementing the other, creating a harmonious whole.

This balance is seen in various elements of Vietnamese culture. From the balanced flavors in Vietnamese cuisine to the balanced approach in social relationships, it's all about creating harmony. Vietnamese people generally avoid conflicts and confrontations, preferring peaceful resolutions that maintain social harmony.

So, if you're interacting with Vietnamese people, remember to bring your calm and balanced self to the table.

The Role of Superstitions and Beliefs

Vietnamese culture is flexible and adaptable, with a fair share of superstitions and beliefs. These range from numerology and zodiac signs to customs around special occasions and life events.

For example, the number 4 is considered unlucky as it sounds like the word for 'death' in Vietnamese. On the other hand, the number 8 is deemed lucky as it signifies prosperity. So, if you're thinking of giving a gift, maybe choose eight sets instead of four.

Vietnamese people also heed the lunar calendar to choose auspicious dates for significant events such as weddings or starting a new business. It's like consulting the weather before planting a new tree, ensuring favorable conditions for growth.

Superstitions also extend to everyday life. For example, don't be surprised if someone refuses to sweep the house at night. It's believed that sweeping after sunset can sweep away good luck.

While these beliefs may not have a logical explanation, they are deeply woven into the fabric of Vietnamese culture. Respecting these beliefs is a way of showing respect for the culture and its people. So, while in Vietnam, let the superstitious winds guide you, and you'll find a culture rich with symbolism and tradition.

With these insights into the Vietnamese way of thinking, you're now equipped to navigate the cultural landscapes of Vietnam. But remember, this is just the tip of the iceberg. The real understanding comes from immersing yourself in the culture, experiencing it first-hand, and learning from your interactions. So, keep an open mind and a respectful attitude, and let the Vietnamese winds of wisdom guide you on this exciting cultural exploration.

1.4 The Role of Family in Vietnamese Culture

We touched on the role of family in Vietnam a little, but considering its significance, let's explore this further. A hierarchical structure, respect for elders, and the principle of filial piety are central to Vietnamese culture.

Let's dig deeper:

The Hierarchical Structure of Vietnamese Families

As we had previously mentioned, each family member has a designated role. This hierarchy often follows the Confucian principle of hierarchy, where roles are defined based on age and gender.

The head of the family is usually the eldest male, who is responsible for making key decisions and maintaining the family's honor.

Following the head, the rest of the family structure unfolds based on age and gender. Each family member is expected to respect and follow the decisions of those above them in the hierarchy.

So, if you're joining a Vietnamese family or interacting with one, remember to be aware of this hierarchy.

It's not about superiority or dominance but about respect and harmony.

The Role of Elders and Respect for Age

In the Vietnamese family, the elders stand at the top. Their role is respected, their wisdom valued, and their experiences treasured. Elders are seen as the custodians of traditions, guiding the younger generations through life.

Respect for elders is a deep-rooted value in Vietnamese culture. This respect is shown in various ways, from greeting the eldest first to seeking their advice on important matters.

This respect for age extends beyond the family to society in general. So, if you're in Vietnam, remember to show respect to elders, be it your Vietnamese boss, your neighbor, or the old lady selling fruits in the market. Besides, a simple gesture of respect can save "face" in Vietnam.

The Importance of Filial Piety

In Vietnamese culture, children are expected to show obedience, respect, and care towards their parents. This duty doesn't end with adulthood. Even as adults, Vietnamese people carry the responsibility of taking care of their aging parents, both financially and emotionally.

Filial piety also extends to ancestors, with regular ancestral worship and rituals.

So there you have it, the Vietnamese family comprises a harmonious blend of hierarchy, respect for elders, and filial piety. As you navigate your Vietnamese cultural exploration, keep this in mind, as it will help you understand the cultural nuances, decode the social interactions, and appreciate the rhythm of Vietnamese life.

CHAPTER TWO

VIETNAMESE SOCIAL ETIQUETTE

Vietnamese social etiquette reflects respect, harmony, and understanding. In this chapter, we will learn all about this, starting with the first essential aspect - greetings.

2.1 Meeting and Greeting in Vietnamese Style

The Traditional Vietnamese Greeting

Picture this. You're walking down a bustling street in Hanoi and spot a local acquaintance. You want to say hello, but wait! A simple wave or a casual "Hey!" won't do here. The Vietnamese greeting is a subtle art, much like the first step of a dance. It's a blend of the right words, the right body language, and the right sentiment.

The most common greeting in Vietnam is "Xin chào," pronounced as "sin chow," which translates to "Hello." But you don't just blurt it out and move on. The greeting is usually followed by the person's title, which could be their first name, their role, or their relationship to you. So, if you're greeting a friend named Linh, you'd say, "Xin chào Linh."

But what about body language? Do you wave, do you shake hands, do you bow? The answer, my friend, lies in understanding the nuances of Vietnamese culture.

The Use of Formal and Informal Titles

Titles play a crucial role in Vietnamese etiquette. They define the dynamics of the interaction, the level of formality, and the respect accorded to the person.

In Vietnamese culture, people are often addressed by a title followed by their first name. The title could be a familial term, even if they're not related to you. It's not uncommon to refer to people around your age as "anh" (older brother) or "chị" (older sister) or older people as "ông" (grandfather) or "bà" (grandmother).

The use of these titles reflects Vietnamese society's close-knit, family-oriented nature. So, the next time you're addressing someone in Vietnam, remember to pick the right title. It's a small gesture but a significant step in the dance of Vietnamese etiquette.

The Importance of Handshakes and Bows

Now, let's talk about the moves and the physical aspect of the greeting. In the Western world, a firm handshake might be the norm. However, in Vietnamese etiquette, the moves are a bit different. Here, the handshake is not just about the grip; it's about the respect and the sentiment it conveys.

When shaking hands in Vietnam, always use both hands. The right-hand shakes, while the left hand gently touches the other person's forearm or elbow. This two-handed handshake is seen as a gesture of respect and sincerity.

What about bows? Do you bow when greeting someone in Vietnam? Yes, bowing is a common gesture, especially when greeting elders or superiors. The bow is usually slight, just a gentle nod of the head, conveying respect and humility.

So, there you have it. Greetings in Vietnam comprises a blend of the right words, the right titles, and the right gestures. So, when you find yourself in Vietnam, remember to incorporate all these aspects.

2.2 Appropriate Behavior at Public Places - Stepping in Tune with Cultural Notes

The Do's and Don'ts at Temples and Pagodas

When visiting temples or pagodas, wearing modest clothing is a must. Avoid shorts, miniskirts, or revealing tops. Instead, opt for long pants, knee-length skirts, and tops that cover your shoulders and midriff. Keep it elegant and respectful.

Remember to maintain a calm and respectful demeanor once you're inside the temple or pagoda. Loud talking or boisterous laughter is generally frowned upon.

When it comes to photography, always ask for permission.

Etiquette in Public Transportation

Navigating through public transportation in Vietnam is like participating in a lively group dance. It's dynamic and energetic and requires a bit of tact and understanding of the local etiquette.

Buses and trains are the main modes of public transportation in Vietnam. When boarding a bus, remember to let the elderly, pregnant women, and those with children board first.

Once you're on the bus or train, refrain from loud conversations or playing music without headphones.

When it comes to seats, always offer your seat to the elderly, pregnant women, or those with children.

Remember, public transportation in Vietnam is not just about getting from point A to point B. It's about being part of the culture, moving in sync with the local norms, and respecting the shared space.

Dress Code and Behavior at Beaches and Pools

Beach etiquette in Vietnam is different altogether. It respects modesty, local norms, and public decorum.

When visiting beaches in Vietnam, modest swimwear is the norm. Avoid skimpy bikinis or revealing swimwear.

Public displays of affection are generally frowned upon. So, save your passionate moments for a more private setting. On the beach, it's more about enjoying the sun, the sand, and the sea while respecting the public space.

When it comes to swimming pools, the same rules apply. Wear modest swimwear, avoid public displays of affection, and respect the shared space.

2.3 Gift-Giving Etiquette - Navigating the Cultural Nuances of Vietnamese Presents

The Significance of Gift-Giving in Vietnamese Culture

In Vietnamese culture, gifts are often exchanged during holidays, special occasions, or social visits. They're also commonly given in professional settings as tokens of appreciation or to celebrate successful collaborations.

Gifts are seen as an expression of kindness and generosity, a way of strengthening relationships, and showing appreciation for the recipient.

Gift-giving in Vietnam also has its unique aspects, which we'll explore in the coming sections.

Choosing the Right Gift

Choosing a gift in Vietnam calls for matching the gift with the mood and ensuring it resonates with the recipient. The choice of gift often depends on the occasion, the relationship with the recipient, and the local customs.

For casual social visits, fruits, cakes, or flowers are common gifts. They're always appropriate and appreciated.

Traditional gifts like sweets, dried fruit, or special holiday foods are preferred if you're visiting during a festival or holiday. They add joy and celebration to the occasion.

When it comes to business or formal scenarios, gifts like souvenirs from your home country, high-quality tea or coffee, or even office items are suitable. They show respect and professionalism.

But remember, it's not so much about the price tag or the grandeur of the gift. It's more about the thought and sentiment behind it. It's about choosing a gift that reflects your appreciation for the recipient and understanding their preferences and customs.

The Art of Giving and Receiving Gifts

Now that you've chosen your gift, it's time to present it. But wait! Giving and receiving gifts in Vietnam is not as simple as handing over a wrapped package.

When giving a gift, always use both hands. This gesture signifies respect and sincerity. And remember to give the gift privately.

When receiving a gift, again, use both hands. It's a way of showing respect and gratitude to the giver. And don't rush to unwrap the gift. It's customary to wait until the giver has left to open the gift.

2.4 Dining Etiquette in Vietnam

The Role of Chopsticks and How to Use Them

In Vietnamese culture, chopsticks are more than just eating utensils. They're tools of communication, symbols of respect, and essentials in dining etiquette. Using them correctly is crucial.

When using chopsticks, hold them towards the end. Avoid pointing at people or things with your chopsticks. It's considered rude.

Never stick your chopsticks upright in your rice bowl. It resembles the incense sticks used in ancestral worship and is considered a bad omen.

Remember, dining etiquette is all about respect, harmony, and understanding the cultural nuances.

The Order of Serving and Eating

When eating, wait until the eldest person starts eating. It's an act of respect.

This respect extends to serving as well. Allow elders to serve themselves first or offer to serve them. It's a simple gesture that adds to the beauty of the culture.

When it's your turn to eat, remember that Vietnamese cuisine isn't just about savoring flavors; it's about savoring the experience. Take small bites, chew slowly, and engage in conversation.

The Significance of Toasting and Drinking Etiquette

No dining dance is complete without a grand finale, and in Vietnam, that finale is the toast. Toasting in Vietnam is not just about clinking glasses; it's a ritual, a celebration of unity and camaraderie.

The toast usually begins with the Vietnamese cheer "Trăm phần trăm!" or "Một, hai, ba, dô!" (One, two, three, cheers!). The toast is led by the host or the eldest person.

If an elder or a superior offers a drink, it's respectful to accept.

So, there you have it: the culture of Vietnamese dining, which marries tradition with etiquette, respect with enjoyment. Remember, mastering Vietnamese dining etiquette takes practice and patience. But once you've grasped the rhythm, you'll enjoy the meal and appreciate its cultural richness.

Next, let's understand Vietnamese business etiquette.

CHAPTER THREE

MASTERING THE RHYTHM OF VIETNAMESE BUSINESS ETIQUETTE

3.1 Vietnamese Business Etiquette

The Importance of Punctuality

If punctuality is considered polite in some cultures, it's essential in Vietnamese business culture. Being late isn't seen as fashionably tardy; it's viewed as a lack of respect for the other person's time.

So, always be on time, whether you're going for a business meeting, a professional event, or even a casual work lunch. If you anticipate a delay, inform the other person as soon as possible. It's a simple act but sets the stage for a respectful and professional relationship, paving the way for strong professional relationships.

The Role of Business Cards

In Vietnamese business etiquette, business cards are not just pieces of paper with contact information; they're more like billboards that advertise your professional identity. They're your opening move, presenting who you are and what you represent.

When giving or receiving a business card, always use both hands. It's a gesture that shows respect and appreciation for the professional relationship.

Also, take a moment to look at the card and read the details before placing it in your cardholder. It's seen as a sign of respect for the person, a gesture that shows genuine concern about the other person's business.

Navigating Business Meetings

If you thought business meetings were all about presentations and discussions, you're in for a surprise. In the Vietnamese business context, meetings are an opportunity to build relationships, understand the business landscape, and align your business goals.

Before the meeting, sending out an agenda is a good practice. It not only helps in structuring the meeting but also shows respect for the other person's time.

During the meeting, maintain a respectful and attentive demeanor. Vietnamese business culture values harmony and respectful communication.

3.2 Navigating Office Hierarchies

The Respect for Seniority and Position

The leader of an organization is the senior-most person in the office hierarchy.

In Vietnamese offices, respect for seniority and position is a pivotal part of the workplace dynamics. It's akin to the hushed silence that permeates the auditorium when the lead dancer takes the stage. The seniors, much like the lead dancers, set the pace, make key decisions, and guide the team.

When interacting with seniors, show deference and respect. Whether it's listening attentively during meetings or waiting for them to initiate conversations, these subtle gestures can set the tone for a harmonious working relationship.

However, this respect for seniority doesn't mean blind obedience. It's more about acknowledging their experience and wisdom while also contributing your ideas and perspectives.

The Role of Consensus in Decision Making

In Vietnamese work culture, decision-making is often like a group dance. Instead of a single lead dancer making all the moves, every team member contributes to the decision-making process.

This approach to decision-making stems from the Vietnamese values of harmony and consensus. It's about finding a balance, a solution that everyone agrees upon.

However, achieving consensus doesn't mean bypassing the hierarchy. The seniors still guide the process but value and consider the team's input.

So, when you're part of a decision-making process in a Vietnamese office, don't hesitate to share your ideas. But remember, it's not about standing out; it's about moving in sync with the team and contributing to the group.

Understanding the Vietnamese Work Ethic

Behind the thriving Vietnamese business scene, there's a strong work ethic. Vietnamese employees are known for their dedication, discipline, and diligence. They take their responsibilities seriously, striving for perfection and are always willing to learn and improve.

This strong work ethic is also reflected in their loyalty to their employers. Vietnamese employees often stay with the same company for years, valuing stability and security and appreciating employers who provide a supportive and growth-oriented work environment.

So, when you step into the Vietnamese business environment, be ready to match this work ethic. Show your dedication, respect the discipline, and commit to your responsibilities. It's not just about the final outcomes; it's about the practice, the learning, and the growth along the way.

In the realm of Vietnamese business etiquette, office hierarchies play a pivotal role. They set the stage for respect, consensus, and strong work ethics. By understanding and adhering to these unwritten rules, you can effectively navigate Vietnamese business culture, ensuring a harmonious and successful working relationship.

3.3 Understanding Work Relationships

The Importance of Building Personal Relationships

In Vietnam, business is not just about transactions and deals; it's about people, connections, and relationships. Building a personal relationship with your Vietnamese colleagues, partners, or clients calls for you to understand their rhythm and synchronize your moves with theirs.

Establishing a personal connection can start with simple gestures like showing interest in their culture, learning a few Vietnamese phrases, or even sharing a meal.

Remember, in Vietnamese business dealings, personal relationships are the key to success. They're not just about being friendly; they're about building trust, showing respect, and understanding the cultural nuances. So, take the time to get to know and understand your Vietnamese counterparts, and you'll find your business relations more enjoyable and successful.

The Role of Networking and Socializing

Networking and socializing in Vietnamese business culture is about interacting with diverse people, learning about their business styles, and creating a network that moves harmoniously with your business goals.

Networking events, social gatherings, or even casual outings are common in Vietnam. They provide opportunities to meet new people, learn about their business, and explore potential collaborations.

These events also provide a platform to understand the Vietnamese business landscape, the trends, the challenges, and the opportunities.

While networking, remember to be genuine, respectful, and patient. Vietnamese business culture values sincerity and long-term relationships over quick deals or immediate gains.

Navigating Office Politics

Like any workplace, Vietnamese offices, too, have their share of politics. It could be about power dynamics, competition, or conflicts. But navigating through these politics is not about outsmarting others or stepping on toes. It's about understanding the dynamics, respecting the hierarchy, and finding a way to contribute positively to the workplace.

Navigating office politics requires emotional intelligence, cultural understanding, and effective communication. It's about choosing your battles, knowing when to voice your opinion, and when to listen. You should clearly understand when to lead and when to follow.

Remember, navigating office politics is not about winning a competition; it's about contributing to a harmonious and productive work environment.

So, there you have it, the essence of Vietnamese work relationships - a culture that values personal connections, networking, and tactful navigation of office politics. Each aspect of this reflects the values of

Vietnamese business culture - respect, harmony, and long-term relationships.

By understanding and following these principles, you can ensure your Vietnamese business experience is not just successful but also enjoyable and enriching.

3.4 The Ballet of Business Meetings and Negotiations

The Importance of Preparation and Agenda

In Vietnamese, business meetings are not just gatherings but a chance to showcase your knowledge, preparation, and understanding of the business landscape. Consequently, rehearsals are paramount. In the business context, this rehearsal translates into thorough preparation and a well-planned agenda.

A well-prepared meeting agenda provides structure, rhythm, and direction to the meeting. It sets clear expectations, outlines the discussion points, and ensures an efficient and productive meeting.

Before the meeting, take the time to research the attendees, the business context, and the cultural nuances. It's like studying the dance style, understanding the rhythm, and practicing the moves. Your preparation will not only help you feel confident but will also show your Vietnamese counterparts that you value their time and the opportunity to work with them.

The Role of Non-Verbal Communication

In Vietnamese, non-verbal communication speaks volumes.

Vietnamese culture places significant importance on non-verbal cues. It could be a respectful bow, a firm handshake, or even the distance you maintain during a conversation. These subtle cues set the tone for interactions.

For instance, maintaining eye contact is seen as a sign of sincerity and trustworthiness. However, avoid prolonged or intense eye contact, which could be perceived as aggressive or disrespectful.

Similarly, your posture and body language can also communicate respect and attentiveness. A straight posture, a respectful bow, and a warm smile can go a long way in building a positive rapport with your Vietnamese counterparts.

By understanding and respecting these non-verbal cues, you can ensure your interactions leave a lasting impression.

Understanding the Pace of Negotiations

Vietnamese business culture values patience, diplomacy, and consensus. Negotiations often involve multiple meetings, discussions, and gradually building consensus.

While negotiating, be respectful, patient, and persistent. Avoid aggressive tactics or high-pressure strategies. Instead, focus on building relationships, understanding their needs, and finding mutually beneficial solutions.

Remember, in the Vietnamese business scene, negotiations are not a competition; they're a collaborative endeavor. By understanding this, you can ensure your business interactions are not just successful but also an enjoyable and enriching experience.

CHAPTER FOUR

CONQUERING THE LANGUAGE MOUNTAIN

ESSENTIAL VIETNAMESE PHRASES FOR EVERYDAY USE

I magine you're in a bustling Vietnamese street market, the air filled with the tantalizing aroma of Phở and Bánh mì, the vendors calling out their offerings, and the locals haggling over prices. Now, wouldn't it be great if you could join in the banter, order your food, or even bargain a bit in the local language? That's exactly what we're going to learn in this chapter. We will equip you with basic Vietnamese phrases for everyday use, turning you from a spectator into an active participant in the vibrant Vietnamese land.

4.1 Basic Vietnamese Phrases for Everyday Use

Greetings and Common Expressions

Let's kick off our Vietnamese language adventure with greetings and common expressions. They're like the first few steps on your hike, setting the pace for the rest of the journey.

"Xin chào" (pronounced "sin chow") is the Vietnamese way of saying "Hello."

To say "How are you?", you'd say "Bạn khỏe không?" (pronounced "ban kweh kohm").

Saying "Thank you" is as simple as saying "Cảm ơn" (pronounced "kam uhn").

And when it's time to say "Goodbye", you can say "Tạm biệt" (pronounced "tam beeyet").

Phrases for Shopping and Bargaining

Now that we've warmed up, let's take on a slightly steeper trail - shopping, and bargaining phrases. These phrases are your map and compass in the bustling Vietnamese marketplaces, helping you navigate your way and score some great deals.

To ask "How much?", say "Bao nhiêu?" (pronounced "bow nyew").

If you find the price too high and want to bargain, you can say "Đắt quá!" (pronounced "dat qwa"), which means "Too expensive!".

If you're happy with the price and want to buy the item, say "Tôi sẽ mua nó" (pronounced "toy se mua no"), which means "I will buy it."

Essential Phrases for Dining and Ordering Food

The next section on our language adventure is dining and ordering food.

To order food, you can say "Tôi muốn một phần..." (pronounced "toy muon mot fan..."), which means "I want a portion of...".

If you're a vegetarian, you can say "Tôi ăn chay" (pronounced "toy an chay"), which means "I eat vegetarian."

To ask for the bill, say "Tính tiền!" (pronounced "tin tyen"), which means "Check, please!".

And that's the gist of it! Your first set of tools to conquer the language barrier.

4.2 Understanding Vietnamese Slangs and Lingo

Popular Slangs Among Young Vietnamese

Let's plunge deeper into our language expedition by venturing into the vibrant world of Vietnamese slang. These slangs, particularly popular among the younger crowd, add a dash of trendiness to the language, much like the hip-hop beats in a classical symphony.

"Chill" or "chill lắm" (pronounced "cheel lam") is a slang that has seamlessly blended into the Vietnamese lingo, taking on the meaning of "awesome" or "great." So, if you find yourself in a trendy café in Ho Chi Minh City and someone asks you how your Vietnamese iced coffee is, flash a thumb up and say, "Chill!"

Another popular slang is "hốt" (pronounced "hawt"), which translates to "grab" or "get." It's often used when talking about buying something or going somewhere. For instance, if a friend invites you to grab a Bánh mì, they might say "Đi hốt Bánh mì không?" (pronounced "dee hawt banh mee khom"), which means "Want to get a Bánh mì?"

Common Vietnamese Proverbs and Their Meanings

Moving on from slang, let's turn our attention to Vietnamese proverbs. These are like the vintage postcards of language, offering a glimpse into the country's culture, wisdom, and life philosophy.

One such proverb is "Có công mài sắt, có ngày nên kim" (pronounced "coh cong mai sat, coh ngay nen kim"), which translates to "With persistence, iron can be turned into a needle." It's a beautiful affirmation of the Vietnamese ethos of diligence and perseverance. Remember this proverb as you navigate your language learning process, reminding you that with persistence, you can indeed conquer the language barrier.

Another proverb that beautifully captures the Vietnamese spirit is "Đi một ngày đàng, học một sàng khôn" (pronounced "dee mot ngay dang, hoc mot sang khon"), which translates to "Travel broadens the mind." It embodies the Vietnamese belief in the enriching power of travel and learning, a mindset you'll find useful as you immerse yourself in the Vietnamese language and culture.

Slangs Related to Food and Dining

As we continue our language exploration, let's stop for a while at the bustling Vietnamese food streets, where language and cuisine cook up a flavorful symphony. Here, food-related slangs are the secret spices, adding a dash of local flavor to your language repertoire.

For instance, "ngon" (pronounced "ngawn"), which literally means "tasty," is often used as slang to express approval or admiration, similar to "cool" or "awesome" in English. So, if someone shows you their new bike, you can say, "Xe máy ngon!" (pronounced "seh may ngawn"), which means "Cool bike!"

Another food-related slang is "chả giò" (pronounced "cha yaw"), which is a type of Vietnamese spring roll. But in slang language, it's used to refer to a person who's lying or making up stories. So, if you catch your friend fibbing, you could playfully say, "Đừng làm chả giò!" (pronounced "doong lam cha yaw"), which means "Don't make up stories!"

You've now added a colorful palette of slang and proverbs to your Vietnamese language canvas. As you continue to learn, remember to have fun in the process. Experiment with the slang, quote the proverbs, and blend them into your everyday language. Before you know it, you'll not just be speaking Vietnamese; you'll be living it!

4.3 The Role of Tone in Vietnamese Language

If the Vietnamese language were a song, the six tones would be its rhythm, adding depth and meaning to each word. Each tone is a unique inflection of the voice, changing the meaning of a word like.

The Six Tones of the Vietnamese Language

The Vietnamese language is relayed by six distinct tones. Each tone represents a different pitch pattern and can change the meaning of a word entirely.

The six tones are ngang (level), sắc (sharp), huyền (hanging), hỏi (asking), ngã (tumbling), and nặng (heavy).

The Importance of Tone in Conveying Meaning

In the Vietnamese language, the dance of tones is not just about musicality; it's about meaning. The same word can have different meanings depending on the tone used.

For instance, the word 'ma' can mean ghost, mother, which, horse, or tomb, depending on the tone used. =

These tones add a rich layer of complexity and expressiveness to the Vietnamese language.

Tips to Master the Tones

Mastering the tones of the Vietnamese language requires practice, patience, and a keen ear. Here are a few tips to help understand Vietnamese tones:

Practice with a Native Speaker: Just as a dance partner can guide your steps and correct your moves, practicing with a native Vietnamese speaker can help you understand and replicate the tones accurately.

Use Tone Visuals: Visual aids like tone diagrams can help you understand the pitch contours of each tone.

Listen and Repeat: Listening to Vietnamese speech and repeating the words can help you get accustomed to the tones.

Record and Playback: Recording your Vietnamese speech and playing it back can help you identify areas of improvement.

Remember, mastering the tones is not an overnight process. But with practice, patience, and persistence, you can grasp it and enrich your language-learning process.

4.4 Navigating the Language Barrier: Charting Your Course through the Vietnamese Language Seas

The Use of English in Vietnam

English, considered the second language in many Vietnamese schools, has become increasingly prevalent, particularly in cities like Hanoi and Ho Chi Minh City. You'll find English being used in hotels, restaurants, and tourist spots.

Don't be surprised to find locals enthusiastic to practice their English skills with you, especially the younger generation. However, be mindful that proficiency levels can vary, and patience is key.

Using Body Language and Gestures

Continuing our learning process, let's turn our attention to the silent language - body language and gestures. They're like currents beneath the surface, unseen but powerful, steering your interactions in the Vietnamese social scenes.

Vietnamese culture values harmony and respect. Non-verbal cues play a pivotal role in conveying these values. A respectful bow, a warm smile, or even the distance you maintain during a conversation can communicate volumes.

However, be aware of gestures that might be considered disrespectful. For instance, pointing with your finger or your foot, crossing your arms, or touching someone's head can be seen as rudeness.

Helpful Tools and Apps for Translation

Our final language aid is the array of translation tools and apps available at your fingertips.

Apps like Google Translate or Vietnamese English Translator can help you translate words, phrases, or even entire conversations.

Language learning apps like Duolingo or Rosetta Stone offer structured lessons, interactive exercises, and pronunciation guides. They're like your navigation maps, providing a systematic route to language fluency.

Remember, while these tools can be incredibly helpful, they're not always 100% accurate. Use them as aids, but trust your instincts, observations, and learning.

And there you have it. We've covered the Vietnamese language and equipped you with phrases, slang, tones, body language, and translation tools.

So, as you keep learning, remember it's not just about reaching the destination; it's about the adventure, the learning, the connections, and the memories you make along the way.

CHAPTER FIVE

DANCING WITH DRAGONS

CELEBRATING VIETNAMESE FESTIVALS AND TRADITIONS

Imagine standing in a vibrant carnival, the air thick with excitement, the streets pulsating with music, and people dressed in their festive best. This carnival, dear reader, is the grand spectacle of Vietnamese festivals. It's a fiesta of colors, sounds, and emotions, a dance of traditions and customs that vividly depicts Vietnamese culture.

In this chapter, we'll twirl through the festive streets, savoring the traditional foods, partaking in the customs and rituals, and immersing ourselves in the exhilarating celebration of Vietnamese festivals. Our first stop on this festive trail is Vietnam's most signif-icant and widely celebrated festival - Tết, the Viet-namese New Year.

5.1 Tết: The Vietnamese New Year

Preparations for Tết

Tết, much like a grand ball, requires meticulous preparation. The preparations start weeks in advance, keeping the entire country busy.

The markets overflow with flowers, fruits, and tradi-tional Tết foods. You can spot families busy cleaning and decorating their homes.

A key part of the Tết preparations is the Kitchen Gods' Day, typically a week before Tết. Vietnamese families believe that the Kitchen Gods ride a carp to Heaven to report on the family's affairs. Families make offerings, burn gold leaf paper, and release live carp into rivers or ponds as a send-off for the Gods. It's like the opening act of the Tết performance, set-ting the stage for the grand celebrations to follow.

Traditional Tết Foods: The Culinary Symphony of the New Year

No celebration is complete without food, and Tết is no exception. The festival brings a culinary symphony that tantalizes the taste buds and warms the soul.

The star of the Tết feast is Bánh chưng, a traditional rice cake made of glutinous rice, mung beans, and pork. Wrapped in banana leaves and cooked for hours, Bánh chưng is a labor of love, a testament to the culinary heritage of Vietnam. Its square shape symbolizes the Earth, and every bite is like savoring a piece of Vietnamese tradition.

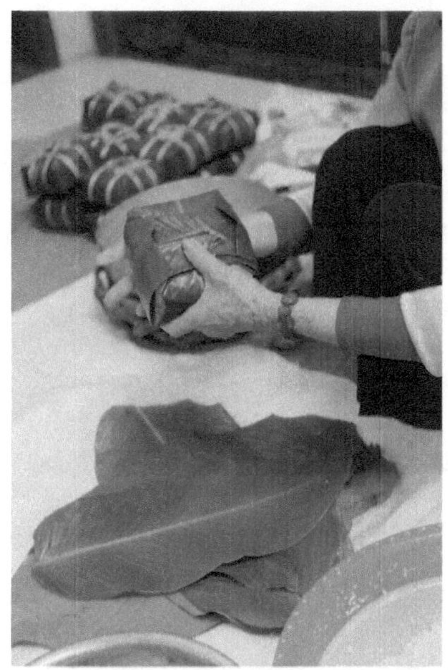

Another Tết delicacy is Mứt, a variety of candied fruits and nuts. Arranged in beautiful boxes, Mứt is not just a feast for the palate but also a treat for the eyes.

Customs and Rituals

The customs and rituals of Tết are the baseline that guides the New Year celebrations. They reflect the Vietnamese values of respect, gratitude, and family bonds.

The first custom is the "Ong Tao" ceremony, the Kitchen Gods' farewell. The family gathers to make offerings and send off the Kitchen Gods to the Jade Emperor. This signals the beginning of the New Year celebrations.

On the eve of Tết, families gather for the "Giao Thừa" ceremony, the transition into the New Year. It's a time for reflection, gratitude, and family bonding. The striking of the gong at midnight marks the arrival of the New Year.

During the first few days of Tết, Vietnamese families visit each other and give children lucky money (lì xì). The first day is spent with the nuclear family, the second with the husband's family, and the third with friends and teachers.

The Lixi tradition, also known as lucky money, holds a special place in Vietnamese culture, symbolizing good fortune and blessings for the upcoming year. This tradition involves giving small envelopes filled with money to children, family members, and friends, often adorned with vibrant red and gold colors, which are considered highly auspicious. Beyond the tangible gift, the act of giving and receiving Lixi is a profound gesture of love and respect, serving as a heartfelt wish for recipients' prosperity and happiness in the year ahead. It is a heartwarming tradition that beautifully embodies hope, prosperity, and the deep sense of family and community that permeates Tet celebrations in Vietnam.

Tết is not just a New Year celebration; it's a tribute to Vietnamese culture. It's a time to honor the past, celebrate the present, and welcome the future.

5.2 Traditional Vietnamese Weddings

The Prelude: The Engagement Ceremony

The engagement ceremony is a vibrant affair, filled with traditional rituals and customs. The groom's family, adorned in their festive best, form a procession to the bride's house, carrying beautifully decorated lacquer boxes as gifts. These gifts usually include betel leaves, areca nuts, tea, cake, fruits, and a roast pig.

The meeting of the two families, the exchange of gifts, and the formal announcement of the wedding date mark the beginning of the impending wedding.

The Wedding Ceremony

The wedding ceremony, or "Lễ Vu Quy," is steeped in traditions, symbolizing the union of not just two individuals, but two families.

The ceremony begins at the bride's house, with the groom's procession arriving with gifts. The couple then proceeds to the ancestral altar, seeking blessings from their ancestors.

Following the ancestral offering, the couple exchanges wedding rings, marking their official transition from betrothed to married.

The Wedding Reception

The wedding reception, or "Tiệc Cưới," is the grand finale of the Vietnamese wedding ceremony.

The reception is a festive affair, with family, friends, and neighbors joining in the celebration. With a lavish spread of Vietnamese delicacies, music, and toasts, the reception is a jubilant celebration, marking the end of a successful wedding.

One of the highlights of the reception is the "Mâm Qua," or gift presentation to the bride's family by the groom's family. Beautifully arranged on red trays, these gifts symbolize fertility, longevity, and prosperity.

The wedding reception is not just a party; it's a celebration of love, unity, and the beginning of a new journey for the couple. As the music fades and the guests depart, the couple is left with beautiful memories, blessings, and the promise of a future together.

As we close this section, remember that the beauty of Vietnamese weddings lies not just in the grandeur but in the traditions, the customs, and the deep-rooted cultural values they uphold. They're not just celebrations; they're tributes of love and commitment, resonating with the graceful rhythm of Vietnamese culture. The steps may seem intricate, and the rituals might appear complex, but once you understand their significance, you'll appreciate their beauty and depth.

5.3 Funerals in Vietnam

Mourning Period

The mourning period in Vietnam serves as a pause in the normal rhythm of life. Known as "Thời Gian Tang Lễ," the mourning period is a time for families to grieve, remember, and honor their deceased loved ones.

The length of the mourning period varies depending on the deceased's relation to the family. For immediate family members, the mourning period may last up to three years. During this time, family members wear simple, often white, clothing and refrain from participating in festive activities.

It's a respectful acknowledgment of the loss, a time to recall fond memories, and a solemn commitment to honor the departed.

Funeral Rituals

The funeral rituals, steeped in tradition and symbolism, guide the family and friends in their final farewell.

The funeral usually lasts for three days, starting with the preparation of the body, which is washed, dressed in white, and laid out for viewing. A picture of the deceased, along with a lit candle, is placed at the head of the coffin, symbolizing the eternal light of spirit.

The procession to the burial ground is another significant ritual. The coffin is carried on the shoulders of male family members, friends, or pallbearers while the mourners follow behind, dressed in traditional mourning attire.

The mourners move in unison, their collective grief and respect creating a powerful ceremony of love and remembrance.

Ancestor Worship

In the Vietnamese culture, ancestor worship is the encore, the tradition that keeps the memory of the deceased alive in the hearts of their descendants. Known as "Lễ Cúng Tổ Tiên," ancestor worship is an integral part of Vietnamese culture.

Ancestor worship rituals are performed regularly, especially on significant dates such as the death anniversary of the deceased and during certain festivals. Families gather to offer prayers, light incense, and prepare a feast, often including the deceased's favorite dishes.

Ancestor worship is an act of remembrance, gratitude, and respect for those who have passed away.

It's a way for families to honor their roots, remember their heritage, and strengthen their bond.

In matters of life and death, Vietnamese funeral customs and traditions guide individuals and families through the process of mourning and remembrance. They uphold the values of love, respect, and reverence for the deceased, creating a harmonious dance of farewell and remembrance.

5.4 Other Important Vietnamese Festivals

The Mid-Autumn Festival: A Lyrical Night of Lanterns and Mooncakes

Let's step into the magical realm of the Mid-Autumn Festival or "Tết Trung Thu," a charming spectacle that turns the Vietnamese streets into a lyrical night of lanterns and mooncakes. Happening on the 15th day of the 8th lunar month, this festival celebrates the fullest moon of the year, symbolizing prosperity and family reunion.

Children take center stage in this festival, lighting up the streets with colorful lanterns. It's like a delightful parade of tiny dancers, their lanterns twirling to the rhythm of the moonlit night. Traditional toys, masks, and lion dances add to the merriment, keeping the festive beat alive.

But what's a celebration without food? The star of the Mid-Autumn feast is the mooncake or "Bánh Trung Thu," a sweet or savory pastry that's as rich in flavor as it is in symbolism. Each mooncake is a delicious symbol of the Mid-Autumn festival, its round shape echoing the full moon and the unity of families.

The Hung Kings Temple Festival

Our festive tour now takes us to the historic "Giỗ Tổ Hùng Vương" or Hung Kings Temple Festival, a grand commemoration of the founding fathers of Vietnam. Held on the 10th day of the 3rd lunar month, this festival is an ancestral tribute, merging the past with the present in a majestic performance.

The beat of this festival resounds in Phu Tho province, where pilgrims from across the country gather to pay homage to the Hung Kings. The ceremonial rituals, the incense offerings, and the shared prayers create a rhythmic flow.

Perfume Pagoda Festival

As we glide further into the festive landscapes, we arrive at the serene "Chùa Hương" or Perfume Pagoda Festival. This religious event, taking place from the 6th day of the 1st lunar month to the last day of the 3rd lunar month, is a tranquil event of spirituality set against the backdrop of picturesque mountains and streams.

The festival's rhythm unfolds as pilgrims embark on a scenic boat ride along the Yen stream, followed by a trek up the mountain to reach the Perfume Pagoda. The serene surroundings, the peaceful chants, and the fragrant incense blend into a harmonious and spiritual festivity that soothes the soul.

National Day

Our festive exploration concludes with "Quốc Khánh" or National Day, celebrated on the 2nd of

September. This day is a grand display of patriotic fervor, commemorating Vietnam's Declaration of Independence from France.

National Day is marked by a spectacular parade in Ba Dinh Square in Hanoi, featuring marching bands, dance performances, and a sea of national flags. Across the country, homes and streets are adorned with the red and gold colors of the Vietnamese flag, painting a picturesque canvas of national pride.

And so, our exploration through the festive landscapes of Vietnam comes to a close. As we move forward on our cultural exploration, let these festivities remind you of the richness of Vietnamese culture. Ready for the next act? Let's continue our exploration!

CHAPTER SIX

SAVORING VIETNAM

A GOURMET GUIDE TO VIETNAMESE CUISINE

Welcome to the world of Vietnamese cuisine—a world where geography shapes the herbs, balance defines the broth, and freshness highlights the produce. We have touched a little on Vietnamese cuisine through the chapters, but let's understand what truly encompasses the flavors, dishes, ingredients, and all!

6.1 A Brief Introduction to Vietnamese Cuisine

Influence of Geography

Vietnamese cuisine is deeply influenced by its geography, with each region offering unique flavors. The North, with its cooler climate and mountainous terrain, features robust dishes influenced by China, such as Phở, a noodle soup with rice noodles, richly flavored broth, and tender slices of meat.

The North, with its cooler climate and mountainous terrain, offers robust flavors. The dishes here are also influenced by China, featuring stir-fries, noodle-based soups, and an abundant use of soy sauce. Think of Phở, the iconic Vietnamese noodle soup, with its delicate rice noodles, richly flavored broth, and tender slices of meat.

As we move towards the central region, the culinary composition becomes more complex. The royal city of Hue, once the imperial capital, is known for intricate dishes like Bun Bo Hue, a spicy beef noodle soup with a fiery broth.

The South, with the Mekong Delta as its culinary signature dish, adds a sweet and sour touch to the cuisine. The fertile delta region is a cornucopia of fresh fruits, vegetables, and herbs, all of which find their way into the southern dishes. Canh Chua, a sour fish soup, perfectly encapsulates southern cuisine with its harmonious play of sweet, sour, and spicy notes.

Balance of Flavors

Balance is central to Vietnamese cuisine, guiding the gastronomic experience with its mix of sweet, salty, sour, bitter, and umami flavors.

Take the quintessential Vietnamese dipping sauce, Nuoc Cham. It's a blend of fish sauce, sugar, lime, garlic, and chili, each ingredient contributing to a balanced and flavorful sauce that enhances the dishes it accompanies.

Even a simple bowl of Phở showcases balance. The richness of the broth, the subtlety of the rice noodles, the freshness of the herbs, the tanginess of lime, and the heat of chili all come together to create a harmonious and delicious dish.

Fresh Ingredients

In the Vietnamese cuisine, fresh ingredients are key. They are the heartbeat that brings vibrancy and authenticity to the dishes.

Take a stroll through any Vietnamese market, and you'll witness this evidence of freshness. From the morning catch of fish and shellfish to the vibrant array of fruits and vegetables, the markets pulsate with the best of each season.

This emphasis on freshness extends to the herbs used in Vietnamese cuisine. Each meal is accompanied by a basket of fresh herbs, also known as "rau thơm." From mint and basil to coriander and lemongrass, these herbs are the high notes in the Vietnamese meals, adding depth, aroma, and a touch of vibrancy to the dishes.

6.2 Navigating a Vietnamese Menu

The Culinary Landmarks

Now, let's explore some typical dishes and the culinary landmarks that define Vietnamese cuisine.

Commencing our exploration, we encounter Gỏi cuốn or Vietnamese spring rolls. These translucent parcels, packed with succulent shrimp, slivers of pork, fresh herbs, and vermicelli noodles, offer a delightful start to your meal.

Moving on, we stumble upon Bún chả, a popular dish from the streets of Hanoi. Grilled pork patties and crispy pork belly slices served over a bed of white rice noodles, with a side of fresh herbs and a tangy dipping sauce.

Next, we explore Cơm tấm, a Saigonese specialty. This dish, featuring broken rice, grilled pork chop, a sunny-side-up egg, and pickled vegetables, offers comfort and familiarity.

Regional Specialties

Next, let's take a detour to the central region, home to the ancient city of Hue. Here, we find Bánh bèo, petite steamed rice cakes topped with dried shrimp, fried shallots, and crispy pork skin, served with a tangy fish sauce. This dish is like the city's historical district, reflecting the region's royal heritage and culinary sophistication.

Traversing to the North, we discover Chả cá Lã Vọng, a Hanoian delicacy. This dish features turmeric-marinated fish grilled tableside and served over a bed of dill and spring onions, accompanied by rice noodles and a shrimp paste dipping sauce.

Venturing south, we encounter Hủ tiếu, a noodle soup that's a breakfast staple in Saigon. With a choice of pork, seafood, or a combination, and served with an assortment of herbs and condiments, this dish offers a canvas of flavors you can customize.

Vegetarian Options

Vegetarian dishes offer a refreshing break from the regular meals. Influenced by Buddhist principles, Vietnamese cuisine offers a plethora of vegetarian options that are as flavorful as they are diverse.

For starters, consider Gỏi cuốn chay, the vegetarian version of spring rolls, filled with fresh herbs, lettuce, and tofu.

For mains, try the Bún chay, a vegetarian version of the noodle dish featuring rice noodles, fresh herbs, and stir-fried tofu or mushrooms.

For dessert, nothing beats Chè, a sweet soup or pudding made with various ingredients like mung beans, black-eyed peas, and tapioca.

And that's your guide to navigating a Vietnamese menu. As you explore this culinary city, remember, it's not just about tasting the food; it's about savoring the experience, understanding the culture, and celebrating the diversity of Vietnamese cuisine.

6.3 Vietnamese Dining Etiquette

Table Manners

Now, let's familiarize ourselves with Vietnamese table manners.

To begin with, seating arrangement plays a key role. The elders or the guests of honor are usually seated first, an act of respect that sets the tone for the meal.

Next up is serving food. Tradition dictates that the eldest person at the table is served first, a respectful nod to the Vietnamese value of reverence for elders.

When it comes to using chopsticks, there's an unwritten code of conduct to follow. Chopsticks should be placed on the table or a chopstick rest when not in use and not left sticking out of a bowl of rice or passed from one person to another. These might seem like small rules, but they contribute to the overall grace of meal times in Vietnam.

Eating is a rhythmic affair, with everyone starting and finishing around the same time; no one is out of step.

A harmonious dining experience is less about the food and more about the people, conversations, and shared laughter.

6.4 Must-Try Vietnamese Dishes

You've probably encountered one or more of these dishes up to this point, but let's explore them a little further.

Phở

Phở (pronounced "fuh") is the heart and soul of Vietnamese cuisine. This iconic noodle soup, with its fragrant broth, tender slices of beef or chicken, and delicate rice noodles, is a harmonious composition that serenades your taste buds. Topped with fresh herbs and paired with a side of lime, chili, and hoisin sauce, Phở can be tweaked to suit your palate. Whether enjoyed as a hearty breakfast or a late-night snack, Phở is a culinary melody that echoes the charm and depth of Vietnamese cuisine.

Bánh Mì

The next meal is Bánh Mì, a flavorful delicacy of East meets West. Picture a French baguette, crispy on the outside and soft on the inside. Now, imagine it filled with an ensemble of Vietnamese ingredients - pickled vegetables, cilantro, and a choice of meat or tofu. This creates a sandwich that's as diverse as the Vietnamese cultural landscape.

Bún Chả

Originating from the streets of Hanoi, Bún Chả comprises succulent grilled pork marinated in sweet and savory flavors, soft rice noodles, and fresh herbs and dipping sauce that add depth to the meal.

Gỏi Cuốn

Next is Gỏi Cuốn, often referred to as Vietnamese spring rolls or summer rolls. Picture a medley of fresh herbs, succulent shrimp, and silky rice noodles, all wrapped up in translucent rice paper. Now, add a dip in a tangy peanut sauce, and voila, you've got Gỏi Cuốn, a fresh summer serenade that cools your palate and teases your senses.

Cá Kho Tộ

Our culinary journey reaches its peak with Cá Kho Tộ, a traditional caramelized fish dish usually cooked in a clay pot. The fish, typically catfish, is simmered in a sweet and salty caramel sauce, resulting in a tender and flavorful dish. Paired with fragrant steamed rice, Cá Kho Tộ is both comforting and indulgent, leaving you satisfied yet wanting more.

As we conclude this chapter, remember that Vietnamese cuisine is more than just a collection of dishes. Each dish tells a story, each ingredient adds a unique note, and each meal celebrates Vietnam's cultural and culinary heritage.

In our next chapter, we'll explore another fascinating aspect of Vietnamese culture—its fashion and clothing styles. Stay tuned; the journey is far from over!

Chapter Seven

Vietnamese Clothing Etiquette

Dress Code for Success and Impress

Vietnamese traditional attire is not just about colors, patterns, or styles; it's about history, culture, and a sense of identity woven into each garment.

In this chapter, we'll explore the exquisite world of Vietnamese traditional attire, understand the nuances of modern Vietnamese fashion, and navigate the dress codes for different occasions. And who knows, by the end of this chapter, you might find yourself twirling in an Ao Dai or strutting in a Non La, blending seamlessly into the colorful tapestry of Vietnamese culture.

7.1 Traditional Vietnamese Attire

Ao Dai: The Quintessence of Vietnamese Elegance

Let's start our sartorial exploration with the Ao Dai, the national costume of Vietnam and a symbol of elegance and grace. Picture a fitted silk tunic, its vibrant colors shimmering in the light, cinched at the waist and flowing down to the ankles. Now, pair it with loose trousers, and there you have it, the Ao Dai.

While the design may sound simple, donning an Ao Dai is like wearing a piece of Vietnamese history. The Ao Dai has evolved over centuries, mirroring the cultural and social changes in Vietnam. From the loose-fitting five-paneled gown of the 18th century to the fitted, body-hugging tunic of today, the Ao Dai's transformation is a testament to the resilience and adaptability of Vietnamese culture.

But the Ao Dai isn't just a historical garment; it's a living, breathing part of Vietnamese life. From school uniforms and office attire to wedding outfits and festival garb, the Ao Dai is omnipresent, echoing the rhythm of daily life in Vietnam. So, whether you're attending a wedding or visiting a temple, donning an Ao Dai can be your way of tuning into this rhythm and stepping into the culture of Vietnam.

Non La: The Signature of Shade and Style

As we continue our sartorial adventure, let's turn our gaze toward the Non-La or the Vietnamese conical hat. Now, you might be thinking, "A hat? What's so special about a hat?" But dear reader, the Non-La is no ordinary hat. It's known for its shade and style, offering practicality and elegance.

Picture a wide-brimmed hat, its conical shape rising gracefully towards the top, the palm leaves woven together in a beautiful pattern. Now, imagine wearing this hat under the tropical Vietnamese sun, its wide brim providing shade and the air vents keeping your head cool.

The Non-La is a testament to the Vietnamese ingenuity and their knack for blending form with function. It's more than just a hat; it's a cultural icon, a symbol of Vietnamese identity. From farmers in the rice fields to vendors in the bustling markets, the Non-La is a familiar sight across Vietnam, adding a touch of grace to the everyday hustle and bustle.

So, whether you're exploring the streets of Hanoi or cruising down the Mekong Delta, donning a Non-La can be your stylish shield against the sun, your fashionable nod to the Vietnamese tradition.

Ao Ba Ba: Comfort and Simplicity

As we twirl further into the world of Vietnamese attire, let's pause at the Ao Ba Ba, a garment that offers comfort and simplicity. Picture a long-sleeved, button-down silk shirt paired with loose-fitting silk trousers. Now, add a touch of color with a contrasting silk belt, and there you have it, the Ao Ba Ba.

While the Ao Ba Ba may lack the grandeur of the Ao Dai or the distinctiveness of the Non La, its charm lies in its simplicity and comfort.

The Ao Ba Ba is a popular choice for casual wear, especially in the southern provinces of Vietnam. Its loose fit and breathable fabric make it perfect for the tropical climate, while its simple elegance adds a touch of style to the everyday ensemble.

So, whether you're visiting a local market or enjoying a leisurely stroll in the countryside, slipping into an Ao Ba Ba can be your way of embracing the comfort and simplicity of Vietnamese life, of swaying to the gentle rhythm of the Vietnamese lifestyle.

And with that, we conclude the first part of our exploration into Vietnamese attire. Remember, as you step into these traditional attires, you're not just dressing up; you're becoming a part of the Vietnamese culture.

7.2 Modern Vietnamese Fashion

Influence of Western Fashion

In the dynamic world of Vietnamese fashion, Western influence adds a contemporary touch to the traditional rhythm. Picture the classic Ao Dai, and its silhouette reshaped into a trendy dress, its silk fabric replaced with denim or lace. This blend of Eastern tradition and Western innovation creates a fusion that mirrors the evolving identity of modern Vietnam.

Western style elements, from ripped jeans and oversized hoodies to tailored suits and little black dresses, have found their way into the Vietnamese wardrobe. But the beauty of this fusion lies in its balance. The Western styles don't overshadow the traditional Vietnamese attire; instead, they harmonize with it, creating unique fashion that resonates with both tradition and modernity.

Street Style in Vietnam: The Improv Jazz

The street style in Vietnam is a reflection of the country's youthful energy, creativity, and individuality.

The street style in cities like Hanoi and Ho Chi Minh City is a diverse mix of global trends and local flavors. Think baggy T-shirts paired with "áo Bà Ba" trousers or Ao Dai tunics worn over ripped jeans. It's a style symphony that plays with layers, experiments with accessories and isn't afraid to break the fashion rules.

Streetwear brands, both local and international, are also making their mark in the Vietnamese fashion scene. From graphic tees and cargo pants to chunky sneakers and snapbacks, the streetwear culture in Vietnam is on the rise.

High Fashion in Vietnam: The Couture

Our fashion exploration concludes with the glamorous world of high fashion in Vietnam, showcasing Vietnamese designers' creativity and craftsmanship on the global catwalk.

Vietnamese designers are making waves in the international fashion scene, and their collections blend traditional motifs, modern aesthetics, and sustainable practices. From reinventing the Ao Dai for the modern woman to creating couture collections inspired by ethnic minority cultures, these designers are putting Vietnamese fashion on the global map.

Fashion events like the Vietnam International Fashion Week and the Vietnam Fashion Fair provide a platform for these designers to showcase their collections, their creativity setting the stage for a breathtaking fashion performance.

So, there you have it - from traditional attires and Western influences to street styles and high fashion, we've journeyed through the Vietnamese fashion scene.

As you step into these styles, remember that fashion is not just about wearing clothes; it's about expressing your identity, celebrating your individuality, and embracing the cultural rhythm that makes you unique. So, keep dancing, keep exploring, and let your style tell your story.

7.3 Appropriate Attire for Different Occasions

Business Attire

In Vietnamese professional life, the right business attire is your glowing spotlight. It's not just about looking sharp; it's about showcasing your respect for the business culture, the occasion, and the people you interact with.

For men, the standard business attire leans towards the formal side, usually a dark-colored suit paired with a light-colored shirt. Ties are common, adding a professional touch to the ensemble.

For women, the business attire ranges from suits and skirts to the traditional Ao Dai. The choice of attire often depends on the nature of work and the work-place culture.

While dressing for business occasions, remember to avoid flashy colors or excessive accessories. In Viet-namese business fashion, subtlety and modesty take center stage.

Casual Wear

Casual wear in Vietnam is all about personal style and comfort. From jeans and t-shirts to shorts and sundresses, it's designed for convenience and ease. Given the tropical climate, light, breathable fabrics like cotton and linen are popular choices, keeping you cool and comfortable throughout the day.

While selecting casual wear, it's important to be mindful of the local culture and customs. Avoiding overly revealing clothes is advisable, especially in rural areas and religious sites.

Formal Wear

For formal occasions, dressing up is an opportunity to showcase your finest attire and style.

For men, a formal suit or a tuxedo is a perfect choice, exuding class and sophistication.

For women, a formal dress or an exquisite Ao Dai can make a stunning statement.

Attention to detail can elevate your style for formal events. Well-matched accessories, tasteful jewelry, and fine shoes add the finishing touches to your ensemble, ensuring a polished and elegant appearance.

7.4 Shopping for Clothes in Vietnam: Strutting Down the Fashion Runways

Tailoring in Hoi An

In the captivating town of Hoi An, a different kind of sound wafts through the air. It's the rhythmic hum of sewing machines, the rustle of silk, the snip-snip of scissors - the symphony of tailoring. Hoi An is like a vibrant fashion studio, its narrow streets lined with tailor shops, each promising a bespoke experience.

Walking into a Hoi An tailor shop is like stepping into a designer's dream. Bolts of fabric in every possible hue, pattern books boasting the latest styles, and tailors ready to transform your fashion fantasies into reality. Whether you fancy a custom-made Ao Dai, a stylish suit, or even a replica of your favorite designer dress, the nimble-fingered tailors of Hoi An can whip it up for you.

The process is simple. First, you pick a style from the pattern books or bring your own design. Next, you choose the fabric, a tactile feast of silk, cotton, and linen. Then come the measurements, meticulously taken to ensure a perfect fit.

Finally, in a day or two, your custom-made outfit is ready for a fitting. A tweak here, an adjustment there, and voila, you're all set to strut down your personal fashion runway.

Shopping Malls in Ho Chi Minh City

From the traditional allure of Hoi An, let's teleport to the buzzing metropolis of Ho Chi Minh City - the stage of modern fashion. Here, towering shopping malls dot the cityscape, their glitzy storefronts beckoning fashionistas to a world of sartorial splendor.

Ho Chi Minh City shopping malls are like fashion orchestras, each store playing its unique note. International brands, local designers, chic boutiques, and trendy fast-fashion - the city's malls are a testament to Vietnam's thriving fashion scene.

Whether you're hunting for the latest sneakers, a beach-ready sundress, or a statement accessory, the city's shopping malls have got you covered.

Markets in Hanoi

Our fashion tour concludes in the charming city of Hanoi, the heart of Vietnamese street style. Here, bustling markets offer a sensory feast of colors, textures, and styles, all at bargainable prices.

From the labyrinthine lanes of the Old Quarter to the lively stalls of Dong Xuan Market, Hanoi's markets are a fashion playground. Silk scarves, embroidered bags, quirky accessories, and even tailor-made clothes - shopping in Hanoi is spontaneous and exhilarating.

But remember, bargaining is part of the market world in Hanoi. It's not just about snagging a good deal; it's a cultural exchange, a playful banter between buyer and seller. So, put on your bargaining hat, flash your friendliest smile, and dive into the vibrant dance of Hanoi markets.

And there you have it. We've explored the fashion runways of Vietnam, visited the tailoring shops of Hoi An, shopped in the malls of Ho Chi Minh City, and bargained in the markets of Hanoi. Each experience, each garment, and each style is a part of the vibrant fabric of Vietnamese fashion, reflecting the country's evolving fashion landscape and cultural richness. Remember, fashion in Vietnam is not just about clothes; it's an expression of identity and a celebration of culture.

As we conclude our look at Vietnamese clothing etiquette, we'll now prepare to explore Vietnamese arts and literature in our next chapter. We'll discover how the creative spirit of Vietnam expresses itself through words, colors, and performances. Stay tuned!

Chapter Eight

Vietnamese Art

Palette of the Past, Canvas of the Future

A picture, they say, is worth a thousand words. But in Vietnam, every stroke of the brush, each carve on the wood, and every weave of the silk is worth a history lesson, a cultural insight, and a story untold. Vietnamese art, with its unique techniques, deep-rooted traditions, and evolving styles, is like a vibrant palette that paints a vivid picture of the country's past and present. In this chapter, we'll dip our brushes into this colorful palette, exploring the fascinating world of Vietnamese art and how it reflects the country's history, culture, and spirit.

8.1 An Overview of Vietnamese Art

Lacquerware

As we step into the gallery of Vietnamese art, let's start with Lacquerware, a traditional art form that's as Vietnamese as the Phở or the Ao Dai. Picture a wooden object, its surface coated with layers of lacquer and intricately decorated with gold leaf, eggshell, and mother-of-pearl.

Now, imagine this object under the light, its glossy finish reflecting a dance of colors, textures, and stories. This, dear reader, is Lacquerware, a glossy Vietnamese art that has been present for centuries.

The process of making lacquerware involves several steps - from coating the wooden object with layers of lacquer and sanding it to create a smooth surface to adding decorations and polishing the final piece. The result is a stunning work of art that's as durable as it is beautiful.

Lacquerware, with its luxurious finish and intricate designs, is a popular form of Vietnamese art, sought after by art lovers and collectors worldwide. From decorative panels and furniture to jewelry and souvenirs, lacquerware brings a touch of Vietnamese elegance to any space.

Silk Painting

Next, we glide into the world of Silk Painting, a delicate ballet of colors and fabrics that captures the essence of Vietnamese landscapes, lifestyles, and legends.

Picture a piece of silk, its fabric as smooth as a calm lake. Now, imagine an artist painting on this silk, their brush dancing on the fabric, their colors seeping into the threads, creating a painting that's as soft as a dream and as vibrant as life. This, my friend, is Silk Painting, a unique art form that blends the softness of silk, the fluidity of watercolors, and the cultural richness of Vietnam.

The beauty of silk painting lies in its subtlety. The colors, instead of sitting on the surface, penetrate the fabric, creating a translucent effect that adds depth and luminosity to the painting. From serene landscapes and bustling street scenes to mythical creatures and historical events, a range of themes finds expression on the soft canvas of silk.

Ceramics

As we continue our art journey, let's turn our attention to Ceramics, a rhythmic symphony of clay and fire that resonates with Vietnamese history and craftsmanship. Picture a lump of clay spinning on a potter's wheel.

Now, imagine the potter's hands shaping the clay, their fingers dancing to the rhythm of the spinning wheel, their touch transforming the humble clay into a piece of art. This is the magic of Vietnamese ceramics.

From the intricate pottery of the ancient Đông Sơn culture and the blue and white ceramics of the Lý dynasty to the glazed terracotta of the Bát Tràng village, the history of Vietnamese ceramics is as rich and varied as the clay it's molded from. Whether it's a stately vase or a humble teacup, each ceramic piece is a testament to the skill, patience, and creativity of the Vietnamese artisans.

8.2 Traditional Vietnamese Music and Dance

Ca Tru

First on our stage is Ca Tru, an exquisite form of ceremonial singing that has been serenading Vietnam for centuries. Picture a small group of performers, their voices harmonizing with the rhythm of the Đàn đáy, a Vietnamese long-necked lute, and the Phách, a bamboo percussion instrument. This, dear reader, is Ca Tru, a graceful dance of voice and instruments that captivates the audience with its poetic lyrics, intricate melodies, and subtle interplay between the singers and the instruments.

The performance is a dialogic dance, with the female singer leading the performance and the spectators (often scholars and intellectuals in the past) chiming in with the occasional phrase or comment. The singer sings and plays the Phách, the beats of which punctuate the flow of the music.

With its elegant performance and intellectual lyrics, Ca Tru is more than just a form of entertainment. It's a ritual, a social event, and a space for cultural discourse, where music, poetry, and intellect dance together, creating a melodious performance that's thought-provoking.

Water Puppetry

Next, let's wade into the world of Water Puppetry, a unique form of Vietnamese puppetry that brings legends and folklore to life on a stage of water. Picture a pool of water, serving as the stage, and wooden puppets, gracefully controlled by puppeteers standing behind a screen. This, my friend, is Water Puppetry, a captivating ballet on water that has been entertaining audiences for nearly a thousand years.

Each puppet, carved from wood and lacquered to make it waterproof, is a dancer in this aquatic ballet. The puppeteers, hidden behind a bamboo screen, control the puppets using large rods submerged under the water. The puppets appear to be moving on their own, dancing on the water's surface, captivating the audience with their graceful movements and expressive performances.

Water Puppetry performances often depict scenes from rural life, historical legends, and folk tales, each performance a dance of tradition and storytelling. Accompanied by a traditional Vietnamese orchestra, the performances are a feast for the eyes and the ears, offering a glimpse into the rich cultural tapestry of Vietnam.

Lion Dance

As we continue our exploration of Vietnamese music and dance, let's leap into the world of the Lion Dance, a spirited dance filled with rhythm, movement, and symbolism. Picture a large, colorful lion, its body animated by two dancers moving in perfect sync.

Now, add the beat of the drums, the clang of the cymbals, and the cheering crowd. This is the Lion Dance, a vibrant performance that brings energy, excitement, and good fortune.

The Lion Dance is a highlight of Vietnamese celebrations, especially during Tết (Vietnamese New Year) and Mid-Autumn Festival. The dance tells a story, often involving a lion chasing a ball, which symbolizes the moon or the sun. The lion's movements, from the blinking of its eyes to the wagging of its tail, are meticulously choreographed, each movement adding to the narrative and the visual spectacle.

The Lion Dance is not just a performance; it's a colorful canvas of culture and celebration and a lively dance that brings communities together, spreading joy, prosperity, and the festive spirit. So, as you witness the Lion Dance, don't just watch the performance; join in the dance, soak in the energy, and embrace the festive spirit of Vietnam.

In the rich culture of Vietnamese music and dance, each aspect paints a vivid picture of the country's cultural richness and artistic flair. From the elegant harmonies of Ca Tru and the captivating ballet of Water Puppetry to the spirited symphony of the Lion Dance, Vietnamese music and dance invite you to experience the country's tradition, creativity, and celebratory spirit. So, let the music guide you, let the dance inspire you, and immerse yourself in the beautiful ballet of Vietnamese music and dance.

8.3 The Richness of Vietnamese Literature

Folk Tales

Now, let's dive into the heart of Vietnam's cultural reservoir with its folk tales, the enchanting narratives that have been whispered from generation to generation. Each tale cradles the wisdom, beliefs, and values of the Vietnamese people in its verses.

The folk tales of Vietnam span a broad spectrum, from moralistic fables and mythical legends to heroic epics and romantic tragedies. Each story is a vividly painted scene on the vast canvas of Vietnamese folk-lore.

Characters such as the clever mouse deer, the ambitious frog, or the virtuous princess come alive in these tales, playing out dramas that entertain, educate, and inspire.

One can't help but get lost in these mesmerizing tales that are as varied as the Vietnamese landscape itself. They capture the vibrant spirit of the bustling markets, the rhythmic hum of the countryside, the serene whispers of the pagodas, and much more. They are a timeless treasure, an essential thread in the Vietnamese literature.

Poetry

The beauty of Vietnamese literature truly shines in its poetry, the soulful ballads that echo with the heart's rhythm and the soul's melody. Just like the Red River's serene flow or the rice fields' rhythmic sway in the breeze, Vietnamese poetry flows with a rhythm that resonates with the pulse of life.

The themes of Vietnamese poetry are diverse as well. From the touching verses of love and longing to the passionate ballads of war and heroism, each poem is a heartfelt exploration of emotions and experiences. They mirror the changing seasons, the ebb and flow of life, the joys and sorrows, and the dreams and realities of the Vietnamese people.

The beauty of Vietnamese poetry lies in its simplicity and depth. Each verse and word is chosen with care and woven together to create poetry filled with emotions.

Whether it's a lyrical ode to the beauty of nature, a soulful sonnet about a lost love, or a powerful anthem of resistance and resilience, Vietnamese poetry touches the heart, provokes thought, and stirs the soul.

Modern Vietnamese Literature

Now, let's turn the pages towards modern Vietnamese literature, the contemporary narratives that reflect the changing landscapes of Vietnam's society and culture. From novels and short stories to plays and essays, modern Vietnamese literature offers a diverse array of genres, each telling a unique story, each echoing with the voice of modern Vietnam.

The themes of modern Vietnamese literature are as varied as the vibrant streets of Ho Chi Minh City. They explore the complexities of urban life, the challenges of modernity, the impact of historical events, and the eternal human themes of love, loss, and longing. They offer a window into the lives of the Vietnamese people, their dreams and struggles, their joys and sorrows, their past and their future.

What makes modern Vietnamese literature intriguing is its ability to weave traditional themes with contemporary narratives. Whether it's a novel exploring the impact of war on a family or a play satirizing the bureaucracy of a government office, modern Vietnamese literature is a fascinating exploration of the human condition set against the backdrop of contemporary Vietnam.

Now that we've explored the vibrant world of Vietnamese literature, we can move forward to acquaint ourselves with some of Vietnam's major cultural institutions. These institutions play a pivotal role in preserving and promoting the rich cultural heritage of Vietnam, offering a wealth of resources for anyone interested in Vietnamese culture.

8.4 Major Cultural Institutions in Vietnam

Vietnam Museum of Ethnology

The Vietnam Museum of Ethnology is like an open book, its pages filled with the colorful narratives of Vietnam's 54 ethnic communities. Located in Hanoi, the museum is a harmonious blend of indoor and outdoor exhibits, each note highlighting Vietnamese traditions.

The indoor galleries house impressive artifacts, photographs, and audio-visual displays. It's like stepping into a time machine, each exhibit transporting you to a different period, community, and tale of Vietnamese culture.

The outdoor area, on the other hand, is akin to a cultural park. Stroll through the life-size replicas of traditional houses, watch artisans at work, or participate in folk games. It's like being part of a live performance, the culture and traditions of Vietnam unfolding around you.

Vietnam Fine Arts Museum

The Vietnam Fine Arts Museum in Hanoi is a vibrant canvas that showcases the artistic genius of Vietnamese artists across centuries. Housed in a former French colonial building, the museum is a compilation of art forms, each gallery with something unique that captures the spirit of Vietnamese artistry.

Step into the world of ancient art and marvel at the stone sculptures, lacquerware, and ceramics. Experience the emotion and turbulence of war through the poignant war-era artworks.

Just celebrate the evolution and diversity of Vietnamese art through contemporary art exhibits.

Ho Chi Minh City Museum of Fine Arts

The Ho Chi Minh City Museum of Fine Arts is a grand stage that hosts a stunning performance of Vietnamese art. Located in a beautiful French colonial building, the museum is a harmonious waltz of art and heritage that offers a captivating glimpse into Vietnam's artistic evolution.

The museum's collection is a visual feast featuring ancient sculptures, traditional handicrafts, religious artifacts, and contemporary artworks. Each exhibit is a step into Vietnamese art, its rhythm resonating with the creative spirit of the Vietnamese people.

From the intricate details of lacquer paintings to the vibrant hues of silk artworks, the museum offers an immersive experience that is both enlightening and inspiring.

Temple of Literature

The Temple of Literature in Hanoi is a timeless treasure that holds Vietnam's intellectual and philosophical heritage. Built in 1070 as a university for the sons of mandarins, the temple is a tribute to Confucian learning and the scholars of Vietnam.

As you walk through the temple, you'll marvel at the stelae of doctors and stone tablets mounted on turtles that honor the scholars of the Imperial Academy. Explore the five courtyards representing the elements of nature and the path to enlightenment.

The Temple of Literature is not just a historic site; it's a living testament to Vietnam's intellectual history. It's a place where the past and the present fuse, celebrating the timeless rhythm of knowledge and wisdom.

Vietnam National Opera and Ballet

The Vietnam National Opera and Ballet in Hanoi is a grand stage where music and dance come alive in a rhythmic performance that celebrates the performing arts of Vietnam.

Housed in a colonial-era building, the opera house is a visual and cultural landmark that resonates with the rhythm of Vietnamese music and the graceful movements of Vietnamese dance.

From classical operas and symphonic concerts to traditional ballets and contemporary dance performances, the opera house hosts a variety of shows that cater to different artistic tastes.

Whether you're a fan of classical opera, love the drama of ballet, or are intrigued by contemporary dance, the Vietnam National Opera and Ballet offers a captivating experience that will make your heart dance to the rhythm of Vietnamese music and movement.

And on that melodious note, we bring this chapter to a close. As we have seen, each museum, each temple, and each performance venue is a thread in the colorful tapestry of Vietnamese culture. These cultural institutions are not just buildings or venues; they're living, breathing spaces where Vietnam's culture, history, and spirit come alive.

They are stages where the past and the present perform a beautiful dance, inviting you to join in and be part of the timeless performance that is Vietnamese culture.

Chapter Nine

Living in Vietnam

Navigating the Nuances of Daily Life

Imagine yourself standing on a bustling street in Ho Chi Minh City. The air is filled with the tantalizing aroma of street food, the buzz of motorbikes whizzing past, and the vibrant chatter of locals. Now, picture this not as a fleeting holiday memory but as a part of your everyday life. Yes, we are talking about living in Vietnam, an experience that is as exhilarating as it is enriching.

In this chapter, we are going to demystify the process of finding a place to live in Vietnam. This is the first step in your journey towards making Vietnam your home. From researching housing options and understanding rental agreements to familiarizing yourself with local neighborhoods, we'll provide the practical knowledge you need to navigate this process confidently.

9.1 Finding a Place to Live: Laying the Foundation of Your Vietnamese Home

Researching Housing Options

The first step in finding a place to live in Vietnam is to research your housing options. Vietnam offers a range of housing options to suit different lifestyles and budgets.

- Apartments: Apartments are a common choice for expats in Vietnam, especially in big cities like Hanoi and Ho Chi Minh City. They come in various sizes, from studio apartments to multi-bedroom units. Many apartment buildings offer amenities like gyms, pools, and 24-hour security.

- Houses and Villas: If you prefer more space and privacy, you might want to consider renting a house or a villa. These are more common in residential districts and smaller towns. Some villas also come with private gardens and pools.

- Serviced Apartments: Serviced apartments are a convenient option for those who prefer the comfort of a hotel with the feel of a home. They come fully furnished and include services like housekeeping, laundry, and sometimes even a personal chef!

- Shared Housing: If you're on a tight budget or simply enjoy the company, shared housing might be the right option for you. It's also a great way to meet new people and split the bills.

A good starting point for your research is online real estate platforms. Websites like Batdongsan, Mogo, and Expat.com list a wide range of rental properties across Vietnam. You can filter your search based on location, type of property, price range, and other preferences.

Understanding Rental Agreements

Once you've found a place that fits your needs, the next step is to understand the rental agreement. A rental agreement in Vietnam typically includes the following details:

- Rent and Deposit: The monthly rent and the security deposit (usually equivalent to one or two months' rent) are clearly stated in the agreement. Make sure to check if the rent includes bills like electricity, water, and maintenance fees.

- Lease Term: The duration of the lease is specified in the agreement. Most landlords in Vietnam prefer long-term leases (one year or more), but shorter terms can be negotiated.

- Payment Method: The agreement outlines the payment method (cash, bank transfer, etc.) and the payment schedule.

- Rules and Regulations: The agreement includes specific rules of the property, such as pet policies, noise restrictions, and maintenance responsibilities.

Before signing the agreement, read it carefully and clarify any doubts with your landlord or real estate agent. Don't hesitate to negotiate terms that you're not comfortable with. Remember, understanding your rental agreement is crucial in protecting your rights as a tenant.

Familiarizing with Local Neighborhoods: Becoming a Part of the Vietnamese Community

The final step in finding a place to live in Vietnam is to familiarize yourself with your local neighborhood. This involves understanding the local amenities, getting to know your neighbors, and learning about the local customs and etiquette.

Take a walk around your neighborhood and locate essential amenities like supermarkets, pharmacies, hospitals, and public transportation stops. Try out local cafes and restaurants, and explore nearby parks and recreational facilities.

Make an effort to get to know your neighbors. A simple "Xin chào" (hello) can be a great conversation starter. Participating in local events and community activities can also help you integrate into the community.

Last but not least, respect local customs and etiquette. Remember, you're not just living in Vietnam; you're becoming a part of the Vietnamese community. So, embrace the local culture, respect the traditions, and enjoy the unique experience of living in Vietnam.

In conclusion, finding a place to live in Vietnam involves a thoughtful understanding of your housing options, a careful review of your rental agreement, and an enthusiastic exploration of your local neighborhood.

Each step brings you closer to making Vietnam your home, becoming a part of the vibrant Vietnamese community, and enjoying the exciting journey of living in Vietnam.

9.2 Getting Around in Vietnam

Public Transportation System

Navigating the rhythmic chaos of Vietnam's bustling cities is an adventure in itself. The public transportation system, with its network of buses, trains, and ferries, is like the pulsating veins of these cities, connecting the urban hubs with the rural heartlands.

In metropolitan areas like Hanoi and Ho Chi Minh City, buses are the most common form of public transportation. With extensive routes and frequent services, they cover almost every corner of the city, making them a reliable and affordable option for commuting.

Trains, on the other hand, are an excellent choice for intercity travel. They offer a comfortable and scenic journey through the countryside, giving you a glimpse of Vietnam's diverse landscapes. The Reunification Express, which runs from Hanoi to Ho Chi Minh City, is a popular train route that offers a memorable travel experience.

If you are seeking a unique commute, ferries are a great option. Particularly in the Mekong Delta region, ferries are used extensively for crossing rivers and canals, offering a charming voyage through the aquatic scenes of Vietnam.

Motorbike Culture

If there's one image that captures the spirit of Vietnam, it's the sight of a sea of motorbikes swarming the streets. Motorbikes are more than just a mode of transportation in Vietnam; they are a way of life.

From running errands, commuting to work, carrying families, and transporting goods, motorbikes are used for almost everything in Vietnam. They offer flexibility, convenience, and a sense of freedom that's hard to match.

Riding a motorbike in Vietnam might seem intimidating at first, given the seemingly chaotic traffic. But once you get the hang of it, it gradually grows on you. Just remember to wear a helmet, follow the traffic rules, and, most importantly, go with the flow!

Pedestrian Safety Tips

Walking in Vietnam, particularly in major cities, can feel like walking a tightrope. With motorbikes zipping past and sidewalks often occupied by street vendors, pedestrians need to be vigilant and cautious.

When crossing the road, the trick is to maintain a steady pace and let the motorbikes maneuver around you. It might seem counterintuitive, but stopping or changing direction suddenly can lead to accidents.

Sidewalks in Vietnam are often used for purposes other than walking. From street vendors and parked motorbikes to small eateries and shops, sidewalks are a bustling microcosm of Vietnamese life. When walking on sidewalks, be mindful of your surroundings and respect the space of the vendors and shopkeepers.

In conclusion, getting around in Vietnam requires both calm and vigilance. Whether navigating the public transportation system, riding a motorbike, or walking the streets, each experience offers a different perspective and slice of Vietnamese life. So, as you chart your course through the Vietnamese landscape, remember to stay safe, respect the local norms, and enjoy the ride.

9.3 Understanding the Cost of Living

Average Living Expenses

Moving to a new country requires a solid understanding of the average living costs. This knowledge will guide your financial journey in Vietnam. To gauge the depth of your monthly expenditure, you need to consider a range of costs, from rent and utilities to food and transportation.

For housing, in the main cities like Hanoi and Ho Chi Minh City, a one-bedroom apartment in the city center may cost you around $500-$600 per month, while the same outside the city center can be about $300-$400. If you opt for shared accommodation or a less urban area, the rental prices can be significantly lower.

Your utilities, including electricity, water, cooling, garbage, and internet, may add up to around $50-$100 per month, depending on your usage and the size of your accommodation. Keep in mind that air conditioning can hike up your electricity bill, especially during the hotter months.

Transportation costs are relatively low in Vietnam. A monthly pass for public transportation is around $10. If you prefer riding a motorbike, the cost of petrol may add up to $10-$20 per month.

Remember, these costs are approximate and can vary based on your lifestyle, location, and personal preferences. They serve as a starting point for gauging the average daily expenditure in Vietnam.

Budgeting for Groceries

Preparing a budget for groceries ensures you enjoy the best of Vietnam meals without straining your wallet.

The cost of groceries in Vietnam is relatively low compared to Western countries. A trip to the local market can fill your basket with fresh fruits, vegetables, and staples for around $20-$30. Supermarkets may be slightly more expensive, but they offer a wide range of local and imported products.

Eating out in Vietnam is also quite affordable. A bowl of Phở or a Bánh mì sandwich from a street vendor may cost around $1-$2, while a meal at a mid-range restaurant can be about $10-$15 per person.

However, if you have specific dietary needs or prefer imported products, your grocery budget may be higher. As always, these figures are rough estimates and can vary based on your dietary preferences and eating habits.

Healthcare Costs

Healthcare is an important consideration when moving to a new country.

In Vietnam, the cost of healthcare can vary significantly based on whether you choose to use public or private medical services. While public healthcare is quite affordable, it's often crowded, and the quality of care may not match Western standards. On the other hand, private healthcare offers a higher standard of care, English-speaking staff, and less crowded facilities, but at a higher cost.

A routine doctor's visit in a private clinic may cost around $30-$50, while a specialist consultation can be about $80-$100. The cost of medications is additional and can vary based on the type of medicine and whether it's local or imported.

To ensure you can afford healthcare costs in Vietnam, it's advisable to have health insurance. Some expats may be covered by their employer's insurance, while others may need to purchase private health insurance. The cost of health insurance can vary based on the coverage, your age, and your health condition.

In conclusion, understanding the cost of living in Vietnam involves gauging daily expenses, creating a grocery budget, and ensuring your healthcare needs are covered. Each aspect plays a crucial role in your financial planning, helping you steer clear of financial strain.

9.4 Staying Safe in Vietnam

Common Scams to Avoid

Let's face reality, no matter which country you move to, you're likely to encounter a scam or two. Think of it as a pothole in the smooth road of your Vietnamese adventure. While Vietnam is generally a safe country, it's always wise to be aware of common scams to ensure your experience remains pleasant and hassle-free.

- Cyclo and Taxi Scams: Some cyclo (three-wheeled bicycle taxi) and taxi drivers might take the scenic route or inflate fares. To avoid this, agree on a price before the journey or ensure the meter is running.

- Street Vendor Scams: Street vendors might quote inflated prices to tourists. Learn to bargain, or better yet, observe local prices before making a purchase.

- Tourist Site Scams: Be wary of fake tourist guides or unauthorized tours. Always book through a reputed agency and verify details before parting with your money.

- Motorbike Rental Scams: If you rent a motorbike, you might be charged exorbitant amounts for supposed damages. Always rent from reputable companies, check the bike thoroughly, and take photos before you ride off.

Remember, staying alert and informed is your best defense against scams.

Emergency Contacts

In the unlikely event that you hit a snag, don't worry. Here are emergency contacts you can reach out to:

- Police: For any security-related issues, the police can be reached at 113.

- Medical Emergencies: For medical help, dial 115 to reach the ambulance service.

- Fire: In case of fire, call the fire department at 114.

- Tourist Assistance: If you need tourist-related assistance, you can reach the Vietnam National Administration of Tourism's hotline at (024) 3923 5948.

Keep these numbers handy because you never know when you might need them.

Health and Safety Precautions

When it comes to your health and safety in Vietnam, it's important to take a few precautions.

- Vaccinations: Before you move, make sure you're up to date on routine vaccines. Additionally, vaccines for Hepatitis A and Typhoid are recommended for most travelers.

- Food and Water Safety: While Vietnamese cuisine is delectable, be cautious of where you eat. Stick to busy food stalls and restaurants where the food is cooked fresh. Drink bottled or filtered water to avoid waterborne diseases.

- Traffic Safety: The traffic in Vietnam can be chaotic. Always use pedestrian crossings, keep your eyes and ears open, and avoid rush hours if possible. If driving, ensure you have a valid license and always wear a helmet on a motorbike.

- Weather: Vietnam's tropical climate can get hot and humid, especially in the summer. Stay hydrated, wear sunscreen, and wear light, breathable clothing.

Taking these health and safety precautions will ensure that your journey in Vietnam is not just exciting and enriching but also safe and healthy. After all, a smooth sail is the best kind of adventure, wouldn't you agree?

As we wrap up this chapter, remember that every journey comes with its set of challenges. But with the right knowledge, preparedness, and a dash of common sense, you can turn these challenges into learning experiences. They're not just obstacles; they're stepping stones that make your adventure all the more exciting and memorable.

As we move to the next chapter, we'll explore even more aspects of living in Vietnam, further preparing you for your big move!

Chapter Ten

Vietnamese Cultural Etiquette

Building Bridges and Making Connections

A delightful Vietnamese proverb goes, "A day of traveling will bring a basketful of learning." And, oh, what a basketful of learning awaits you in Vietnam, especially when it comes to building relationships.

Whether it's making friends, understanding body language, navigating romantic relationships, or building trust with colleagues, every interaction is an opportunity to learn, connect, and deepen your understanding of Vietnamese culture. So, let's discover the treasures of Vietnamese social etiquette.

10.1 Making Friends in Vietnam

Socializing Opportunities

While the hustle and bustle of Vietnamese cities can be exhilarating, it's the people who truly make the heart of Vietnam beat. And there's no better way to experience the warmth and vibrancy of Vietnamese culture than by making local friends.

Vietnam offers a plethora of socializing opportunities to connect with locals. From language exchange meetups and cooking classes to community events and volunteer programs, these platforms provide a relaxed and informal setting to strike up conversations and foster friendships. For instance, joining a Vietnamese cooking class doesn't just teach you how to make a mean Phở, it also serves up a chance to bond with locals over a shared love for food.

Vietnamese Hospitality

If there's one thing that stands out in Vietnam, it's the hospitality of its people. Vietnamese people are incredibly welcoming and friendly, and making friends often feels as natural as the flow of the Mekong River.

In Vietnam, friendships are not just casual social constructs; they are valued relationships often treated with the same regard as familial ties. Invitations to homes are common, and don't be surprised if your new friends are keen to introduce you to their family or invite you to a family gathering. Embrace these opportunities as they strengthen your friendship and offer a unique insight into Vietnamese family life.

10.2 Understanding Vietnamese Body Language

Respectful Gestures

As we previously mentioned, body language is vital in Vietnamese social interactions.

We have covered basic greetings, so let's move on to the art of addressing someone.

Vietnamese culture places great importance on addressing people correctly. Using the right pronoun for "you" based on age and gender is essential. But there's a visual cue here too. When talking to someone older or of higher status, slightly lowering your head is a sign of respect.

Handling objects, especially money or gifts, with both hands is another respectful gesture in Vietnamese culture. It subtly communicates your respect towards the person and the object.

Non-Verbal Communication

Beyond respectful gestures, there's a whole world of non-verbal communication in Vietnam that silently speaks volumes.

Maintaining eye contact is seen as a sign of sincerity and respect in Vietnamese culture. However, prolonged eye contact can be considered confrontational, especially with someone of a higher status or of the opposite gender.

Spatial awareness is another subtle aspect of Vietnamese body language. Personal space is highly valued, and it's important to maintain a respectful distance when interacting with others, especially those of the opposite gender.

Facial expressions, too, play a key role in non-verbal communication. Vietnamese people often rely on facial cues to understand emotions and intentions. A smile, a frown, or a raised eyebrow can convey a whole range of emotions, making the face a vital instrument in Vietnamese body language.

In conclusion, understanding Vietnamese body language is like learning a silent language. It's a crucial part of your social toolkit, helping you build respectful relationships, avoid cultural faux-pas, and truly immerse yourself in Vietnamese culture. Remember, it's not just about what you say but how you say it.

10.3 Navigating Romantic Relationships

Dating Etiquette

In Vietnam, dating is seen as a serious commitment, often leading to marriage. Casual dating is less common, particularly in the more traditional parts of the country. When a Vietnamese person agrees to date you, it usually means they see a future with you. So, tread carefully and make sure you're clear about your intentions.

In the early stages of dating, modesty and subtlety are highly valued. Public displays of affection are usually avoided, especially in public areas or in front of family members. Holding hands is fine, but anything more than that is best saved for private moments.

Respect is an important part of Vietnamese dating etiquette. Respect for the person you're dating, respect for their family, and respect for their culture. Small gestures like greeting and thanking them in Vietnamese, showing interest in their culture, and being punctual can go a long way in showing your respect.

Family Involvement

In Vietnamese relationships, family plays a pivotal role.

Family values are deeply ingrained in Vietnamese culture. If you're dating a Vietnamese person, you'll likely meet their family early in the relationship. This isn't something to be nervous about. It's an opportunity to get to know your partner better and to show respect towards their family.

Remember to bring a small gift as a token of respect when meeting their family. This could be a box of fruit or a traditional Vietnamese dessert. Greet the elders first, as this is a sign of respect in Vietnamese culture.

In the eyes of a Vietnamese family, dating their son or daughter means you're considering marriage. So, if you're invited to a family gathering, it's a sign that your relationship is serious.

From here, the next stage is engagement or marriage, as covered before.

10.4 Building Trust with Vietnamese Colleagues

Workplace Etiquette

Punctuality is highly valued in Vietnamese work culture. Arriving on time for meetings or work events is seen as a sign of respect and professionalism.

Addressing seniors and superiors by their correct titles is another key aspect of Vietnamese workplace etiquette.

Small gestures, like offering a firm handshake, maintaining eye contact during conversations, or even a polite nod, can go a long way in demonstrating your respect and professionalism.

Relationship Building Activities

In the Vietnamese workplace, relationship-building activities enable colleagues to come together and interact.

Team lunches or dinners are a common way to strengthen workplace relationships in Vietnam.

Company outings or team-building retreats are another popular relationship-building activity in Vietnam. These events are a platform for team members to interact outside the office environment, engage in fun activities, and build a stronger team spirit.

Through these relationship-building activities, you can build trust with your Vietnamese colleagues, fostering a harmonious work environment.

Understanding Hierarchies

Vietnamese work culture is hierarchical, with seniority and position playing a significant role. Decisions are often made at the top and flow down through the ranks.

However, understanding hierarchies in the Vietnamese workplace goes beyond knowing who's in charge. It's about recognizing the role and value of each team member, respecting their contributions, and collaborating effectively to create a harmonious performance.

As you navigate the workplace dynamics in Vietnam, remember that building trust with your colleagues requires understanding workplace etiquette, participating in relationship-building activities, and respecting the hierarchies. By mastering these aspects, you can contribute to a harmonious work environment where trust, respect, and collaboration create an effective collaboration of professional success.

We've now explored the social landscape of Vietnam, from making friends and understanding body language to navigating romantic relationships and building trust with colleagues. Each aspect is a vital part of your cultural acclimatization, helping you build bridges, make connections, and truly immerse yourself in the Vietnamese way of life.

As we turn the pages of this guide, we're not just learning about Vietnam; we're experiencing it. We're not just understanding the culture; we're living it. And as we do, we realize that a country's culture is not just about its traditions, customs, or etiquette. It's about its people - their warmth, their hospitality, their resilience, and their spirit. That's the real heart of Vietnam, the soul of its culture, and the essence of its charm.

CHAPTER ELEVEN

MAKING PROFESSIONAL MOVES

MASTERING THE JOB MARKET IN VIETNAM

Living and working in Vietnam sounds intriguing, doesn't it? Well, your professional adventure in Vietnam is not just a pipe dream; it's a tangible goal that you can achieve with the right knowledge and strategies. So, let's roll up our sleeves, sharpen our skills, and dive into the vibrant job market of Vietnam.

11.1 Finding a Job in Vietnam

Like a well-stocked market in Vietnam, the job market offers a variety of roles across sectors. To pick the right job, you need to understand what's on offer, know where to look, and make your application stand out. It's like buying the best produce from a local market; you need to know what's in season, where to find the freshest batch, and how to pick the best ones.

Popular Job Sectors for Expats

Working in Vietnam as an expat opens up a plethora of opportunities across sectors. Here are some of the popular job sectors for expats in Vietnam:

- Education: Teaching English is a hot commodity in Vietnam. From language centers and international schools to private tutoring, there are numerous opportunities for native English speakers to teach English. Other teaching opportunities include subjects like science, mathematics, and humanities in international schools.

- Information Technology: The tech industry in Vietnam is booming. As the country becomes a hub for startups and tech companies, opportunities for software engineers, IT consultants, and tech project managers are on the rise.

- Tourism and Hospitality: Vietnam is a popular tourist destination with its stunning landscapes and rich cultural heritage. This creates jobs in hotels, travel agencies, tour operators, and restaurants. Roles can range from hotel management and tour guiding to restaurant service and culinary arts.

Job Search Platforms

Just as you would visit different markets for different goods, you'll need to explore various job search platforms to find the right job in Vietnam. Here's where you can start:

- Online Job Portals: Websites like Vietnam-Works, JobStreet, and CareerBuilder offer a wide range of job listings across sectors. You can filter jobs by location, industry, and job level.

- LinkedIn: LinkedIn is a valuable resource for job searching and networking. Many companies post job vacancies on their LinkedIn pages, and the platform allows you to network with professionals in your field.

- Expatriate Communities: Online expatriate communities such as Expat.com and Inter-Nations often have job boards and forums where job vacancies are posted.

- Company Websites: If you have specific companies in mind, check out their websites for job listings. Many companies prefer to post job vacancies directly on their websites.

Resume and Interview Tips

Just as a skillful vendor knows how to display their goods attractively, you must know how to effectively present your skills and experiences. Here are some tips for your resume and interview:

- Resume: Keep your resume clear, concise, and tailored to the job you're applying for. Highlight your relevant skills, experiences, and achievements. For instance, if you're applying for a teaching job, emphasize your teaching experience, certifications, and any experience living abroad.

- Cover Letter: Your cover letter should complement your resume, not repeat it. Use it as an opportunity to express your interest in the role, explain why you're a good fit, and showcase your familiarity with the company and the Vietnamese market.

- Interview: If you're invited for an interview, prepare by researching the company and the role. Practice answering common interview questions and prepare some questions to ask the interviewer. On the day of the interview, dress professionally, be punctual, and remember to show enthusiasm for the role and the opportunity to work in Vietnam.

Nailing the Job Search Process

Here's a quick checklist to help you navigate the job search process in Vietnam:

- Identify the job sectors that align with your skills and interests.

- Explore various job search platforms to find job listings.

- Tailor your resume and cover letter for each job application.

- Prepare for the interview by researching the company and rehearsing your answers.

- Follow up after the interview to express your

continued interest in the role.

In conclusion, finding a job in Vietnam is like shopping at a Vietnamese market. You need to know what's in demand, where to find it, and how to negotiate your way to a successful deal.

With the right strategies, you can navigate the job market effectively, secure a job that suits your skills and interests, and embark on an exciting professional adventure in Vietnam.

11.2 Understanding Vietnamese Work Culture

Work Hours and Holidays

Life in Vietnam moves to its own rhythm, and the work culture is no exception. The typical work week in Vietnam stretches from Monday to Friday, with business hours usually running from 8 AM to 5 PM, with a lunch break in between. However, it's not unusual to see Vietnamese employees stretching their workday beyond these hours, a testament to their dedication and hard work.

But don't worry, it's not all work and no play. Vietnamese employees enjoy several public holidays throughout the year, offering them a much-needed break to relax, spend time with family, or even travel. The most significant of these holidays is Tết, or the Vietnamese New Year. Falling in late January or early February, Tết is a festive and joyous time when businesses close for at least three days, and people get together with their families to celebrate the beginning of a new lunar year.

Office Etiquette

Step into a Vietnamese office, and you'll find a collaborative environment rooted in respect, harmony, and hierarchy. One of the first things you'll notice is the importance placed on titles. Addressing colleagues by their title followed by their first name is standard practice and a sign of respect. So don't hesitate to flaunt your title, whether it's Mr, Ms, or Dr; it's not considered pretentious but rather a mark of professional identity.

Another key aspect of Vietnamese office etiquette is the deference to seniors and superiors. Decisions are often made at the top and flow down the hierarchy, and open disagreement with superiors is generally avoided. Instead, expressing your opinions diplomatically and at the appropriate time is appreciated.

Business Meeting Norms

Vietnam business meetings are like synchronized swimming events: coordinated, structured, and respectful. They are an essential part of professional life, a platform for decision-making, brainstorming, and information sharing.

Before you dive into a Vietnamese business meeting, remember that punctuality is highly valued. Arriving late can be perceived as disrespectful, so ensure you're on time, if not early.

Once the meeting begins, maintain a formal and respectful demeanor. Interrupting others, especially superiors, is a big no-no. Instead, wait for your turn to speak and voice your thoughts politely. If you disagree with someone, express your disagreement tactfully to maintain harmony and respect.

Moreover, it should be noted that decision-making in Vietnamese business culture often involves a consensus. Decisions are usually made after thorough discussion and agreement among all members, reflecting the values of harmony and unity in Vietnamese culture.

By being aware of work hours, respecting office etiquette, and following business meeting norms, you can easily and confidently navigate your professional life in Vietnam.

11.3 Building a Professional Network in Vietnam

Networking Events

In the vibrant canvas of Vietnam's professional scene, networking events bring together different professionals, each bringing their unique perspectives, ideas, and experiences to the table. These events are the melting pots where professionals from diverse sectors come together, fostering collaborations, sparking ideas, and nurturing connections.

Whether it's a business conference, a trade fair, a seminar, or a social mixer, each networking event offers a unique platform to meet like-minded professionals, learn about industry trends, and showcase your skills.

When attending these events, remember to put your best foot forward. Dress professionally, be prepared with your elevator pitch, and carry plenty of business cards. Be proactive in starting conversations, but also be a good listener. Remember, networking is not just about talking; it's about engaging in meaningful conversations and building mutually beneficial relationships.

Professional Associations

In Vietnam's professional world, professional associations are like the guilds of yore, the brotherhoods and sisterhoods of modern professionals. They are the platforms where professionals within a particular sector come together to share knowledge, advocate for their profession, and provide support to each other.

From sectors as diverse as business and engineering to education and healthcare, there's a professional association for almost every field in Vietnam. These associations organize regular events, seminars, and workshops, offering members a platform to learn, network, and contribute to their profession.

Joining a professional association not only enhances your professional development but also boosts your credibility in your field. It's like earning a badge of honor that signifies your commitment to your profession and your dedication to continuous learning.

Social Media Networking

In the digital age, professional networking is not just confined to physical events or associations; it has found a new home in the virtual world of social media. Platforms like LinkedIn, Facebook, and even Twitter have transformed into digital villages where professionals from around the globe come together to connect, collaborate, and converse.

Social media lets you connect with professionals from your field, join industry-specific groups, participate in discussions, and stay updated with industry news. You can showcase your skills, share your insights, and even find job opportunities.

When networking on social media, remember to maintain a professional demeanor. Keep your profile updated, share relevant content, and engage in discussions respectfully. Just as in face-to-face interactions, the key to successful social media networking is to be genuine, respectful, and engaging.

In essence, building a professional network in Vietnam is like nurturing a garden. You plant the seeds of connection, water them with meaningful interactions, and gradually watch them grow into a thriving network.

Whether you're attending a networking event, joining a professional association, or connecting with professionals on social media, each interaction is an opportunity to enrich your professional brand.

11.4 Tips for Successful Business Negotiations

Negotiation Style

Navigating business negotiations in Vietnam requires an understanding of the local negotiation style. Vietnamese business negotiations are typically formal, respectful, and consensus-driven.

The initial meetings are usually reserved for building relationships, earning trust, and understanding each other's expectations. During this phase, it's crucial to demonstrate respect and patience. Avoid aggressive sales tactics or hard bargaining strategies. Instead, focus on building a rapport, understanding the other party's needs, and establishing a foundation of mutual respect and trust.

Decision-Making Process

Once the rapport is established, the focus shifts to the decision-making process. In Vietnamese culture, decision-making is often a group process.

Vietnamese companies often make decisions based on consensus. Proposals and ideas are carefully evaluated, and everyone's opinion is taken into account. This process may take some time, but it ensures that all perspectives are considered, and the final decision is in the group's best interest.

During this phase, it's important to be patient, understanding, and responsive. Provide detailed information, answer questions clearly, and be prepared for thorough discussions. Remember, it's not just about getting the deal done; it's about ensuring that the deal benefits all parties involved.

Follow-up Etiquette

Once the negotiation is over and the decision is made, this is where follow-up etiquette comes into play. In Vietnamese business culture, follow-up communication is vital to ensure that all parties are on the same page and that the agreed-upon tasks are being carried out.

A formal letter or email summarizing the main points of the negotiation, the final decision, and the next steps can be a good start. It serves as a written record of the negotiation and provides clarity on what has been agreed upon.

In the subsequent days, keep the lines of communication open. Update the other party on the progress of the tasks, discuss any issues or challenges, and provide support where needed. This not only ensures the successful implementation of the decision but also strengthens the business relationship.

In business negotiations in Vietnam, each part - understanding the negotiation style, navigating the decision-making process, and following up effectively - plays a crucial role.

The curtain falls on our exploration of professional life in Vietnam. As the spotlight dims, we are left with valuable insights, practical strategies, and a deeper understanding of the Vietnamese job market, work culture, and professional networking. These are not just tips or guidelines; they are keys to unlocking a world of opportunities, tools to build bridges of understanding, and steps to dance to the rhythm of success in Vietnam.

Chapter Twelve

Vietnamese Legal Etiquette

Staying on the Right Side of the Law

Imagine you are cruising along the bustling streets of Ho Chi Minh City on your newly rented motorbike. The wind is in your hair, the city's energy is pulsating through your veins, and the mouth-watering aroma of street-side Phở is teasing your senses. Just when you think you've got the hang of navigating the Vietnamese way of life, a traffic cop flags you down. Uh-oh!

Let's face it. No matter how well you blend in, savoring the Phở, or nailing the language, understanding the local laws of a foreign land is a different ball game altogether. It's like trying to ride a motorbike for the first time. Without the right knowledge and guidance, it can feel overwhelming, if not downright challenging. But don't fret! This chapter will serve as your trusty roadmap, guiding you through the essential laws for foreign residents in Vietnam.

12.1 Basic Laws for Foreign Residents

Visa Regulations

Before you can soak up the Vietnamese culture or explore its breathtaking landscapes, you need to cross the first legal hurdle - obtaining a visa. While the specific requirements may vary based on your nationality and purpose of visit, here are some general guidelines to help you navigate the Vietnamese visa regulations:

- Tourist Visa: If you're planning a short-term stay in Vietnam for tourism, you can apply for a tourist visa. It's typically valid for 30 days but can be extended if you wish to prolong your stay.

- Business Visa: If you're visiting Vietnam for business purposes or considering working in Vietnam, you'll need a business visa. It's generally valid for up to a year, and you may need a sponsor letter from a business partner in Vietnam.

- Work Permit: If you've secured a job in Vietnam, your employer will usually assist you in obtaining a work permit. The permit is valid for up to two years and requires documents like a health check, a criminal background check, and proof of professional qualifications.

Remember, visa regulations can change, and it's always best to check the latest information from official sources or consult with a legal expert.

Housing Laws

Once you've set foot in Vietnam, the next step is finding a place to call home. While house hunting in a new country can be an adventure, it's important to understand the housing laws in Vietnam to ensure a smooth and legal transition:

- Rental Agreement: When you rent a house or an apartment in Vietnam, you'll need to sign a rental agreement with the landlord. This agreement outlines the terms and conditions of the lease, including the rent amount, duration of the lease, and tenant's responsibilities.

- Registration: Foreign residents in Vietnam are required to register their place of residence with the local police. Usually, your landlord will take care of this process, but it's a good idea to confirm this with them when signing the lease.

- Property Rights: While foreign residents can

lease property in Vietnam, property owner-ship laws are more complex. Foreigners can own apartments and houses in Vietnam for a period of 50 years, but there are restrictions on the total number of properties that for-eigners can own.

Employment Laws

You've got your visa, found a place to live, and now you're ready to dive into work. But before you do, it's crucial to understand the employment laws in Vietnam:

- Work Contracts: If you're working in Viet-nam, you'll need to sign a work contract with your employer. This contract outlines the terms and conditions of your employ-ment, including your job role, salary, work-ing hours, and employee benefits.

- Taxes: As a foreign worker in Vietnam, you are subject to Vietnamese tax laws. You'll need to pay personal income tax on your earnings in Vietnam, with the tax rate depending on your income level.

- Social Insurance: Vietnam's labor law requires both employers and employees to contribute to social insurance. The insurance provides benefits for sickness, maternity, workplace accidents, retirement, and death.

Navigating a foreign country's legal landscape can feel like deciphering an unfamiliar language. But with the right knowledge and resources, you can understand the basics and ensure that your stay in Vietnam is smooth, enjoyable, and, most importantly, legal. So keep this guide handy, stay informed, and enjoy your Vietnamese adventure, knowing that you're on the right side of the law.

12.2 Understanding the Vietnamese Legal System

Court System

The Vietnamese court system has three main levels. The first is at the district level, handling the majority of cases, including civil, administrative, and certain criminal cases. It's like the starting point of the maze, where most legal disputes begin their journey.

The next level is the provincial court, which hears appeals from the district courts and handles more serious criminal cases. This court is akin to the decision point in the maze, where you choose the path that could lead closer to the exit.

The final level is the Supreme People's Court, the highest court in the land. It supervises the lower courts and handles appeals from the provincial courts. Think of this court as the exit of the maze, the final destination where legal disputes reach their conclusion.

Legal Representation

Venturing into legislature alone is daunting in any circumstance. Having a guide makes the journey less intimidating. Here, an attorney serves as this guide, helping you understand the twists and turns of the system with their expertise.

In Vietnam, attorneys are members of the Vietnam Bar Federation, which oversees the legal profession. An attorney's role is to provide legal advice, represent clients in court, and protect their client's rights and interests.

Selecting the right attorney is crucial. Look for someone with expertise in your specific legal matter, a good reputation, and a clear communication style. Remember, your attorney is your ally in the legal maze, so choose wisely.

Dispute Resolution

In every maze, there's often a shortcut - a secret path that bypasses the twists and turns and leads straight to the exit. In the legal maze, alternative dispute resolution (ADR) methods, such as mediation and arbitration, serve as these shortcuts.

Mediation is a process where a neutral third party, the mediator, helps the disputing parties reach a mutually satisfactory resolution. It's a voluntary, confidential process that prioritizes cooperation over confrontation. Consider mediation a secret passage, helping you reach a resolution without going through the entire legal process.

Arbitration, on the other hand, is more formal. An arbitrator listens to both sides and makes a binding decision. It's similar to a court proceeding but less formal and more flexible. Arbitration can be seen as a faster route, bypassing some of the complexities of a court trial.

In conclusion, understanding the Vietnamese legal system involves understanding the structure of the court system, securing the right legal representation, and considering alternative dispute resolution methods. With this knowledge, you can confidently navigate the legal system, ensuring your stay in Vietnam is enjoyable and legally sound.

12.3 Rights and Responsibilities of Foreign Workers

Labor Laws

Take the bustling streets of Hanoi, replace the buzzing motorbikes with bustling businesses, and replace the street vendors with corporate entities. You've got a pretty good idea of the Vietnamese labor market. It's dynamic, it's diverse, and it's governed by a set of labor laws that set the stage for your professional performance in Vietnam.

A legal framework known as the Labor Code governs your rights and responsibilities in the workplace. It's a bit like the director of your professional performance, guiding you on what to do and how to do it.

The Labor Code outlines the terms and conditions of employment contracts, working hours, overtime, rest periods, wages, and workplace safety. Here's what you need to know:

- Employment Contracts: An employment contract will govern your relationship with your employer. This legal document outlines the terms of your employment, including your job role, salary, and working hours.

- Working Hours and Overtime: The standard work week in Vietnam is 48 hours, spread over six days. If your role requires you to work beyond these hours, you are entitled to overtime pay.

- Wages: Your wage or salary must be agreed upon in your employment contract. The Labor Code mandates that wages must be paid on time and in full.

- Workplace Safety: Employers are required to ensure a safe and healthy work environment. This includes providing necessary safety equipment and conducting regular safety training.

Tax Obligations

Working in Vietnam, you're not just earning your wages, but you're also contributing to the country's economic stability through your tax obligations.

As a foreign worker in Vietnam, you are required to pay personal income tax. The tax rates are progressive, which means they increase as your income does. The rates range from 5% for income up to 5 million VND per month to 35% for income over 80 million VND per month.

Your employer will typically deduct these taxes from your salary and pay them to the tax authorities on your behalf. However, it's a good idea to familiarize yourself with the tax rates and ensure that the correct amount is being deducted.

Social Security Benefits

Social security benefits are there to support you in times of need. In Vietnam, both employers and employees contribute to the Social Security Fund, which provides benefits in case of sickness, maternity, workplace accidents, retirement, and death.

As a foreign worker in Vietnam, you are required to contribute to the social security fund if you have a work permit, a practice certificate, or a practice license issued by Vietnamese authorities and have an indefinite-term labor contract or a definite-term labor contract of three months or more with an employer in Vietnam.

The contribution rate for employees is 8% of their salary. Social Security contributions are typically deducted from your salary by your employer and paid to the Social Security authorities.

In conclusion, as a foreign worker in Vietnam, understanding your rights and responsibilities is key to a successful and fulfilling professional life. From labor laws to tax obligations and social security benefits, each aspect plays a critical role in shaping your work experience in Vietnam.

12.4 Things to Avoid in Vietnam

Drug Laws

Though Vietnam's vibrant energy can be intoxicating, it's essential to remember that actual intoxication, particularly involving drugs, is a strict no-go zone. Vietnam has stringent drug laws, with severe penalties for drug trafficking and possession. Even a small amount of a prohibited substance could land you in hot water - we're talking hefty fines, long-term imprisonment, or, in extreme cases, even the death penalty.

So, the message here is loud and clear – drugs and Vietnam mix as well as oil and water. Staying drug-free isn't just about obeying the law; it's about respecting the cultural norms and safeguarding your health and well-being.

Traffic Violations

Navigating Vietnam's streets can be a thrilling experience, with their ceaseless flow of motorbikes and the seemingly chaotic symphony of horns. However, amidst this organized chaos, traffic laws exist and are enforced.

Ignoring red lights, not wearing a helmet while riding a motorbike, or driving under the influence are all serious violations that can result in fines or even a revoked driving license.

Therefore, when you're on the road, make safety your priority. Follow traffic rules, wear a helmet, and avoid drinking and driving.

Cultural Taboos

Every culture has its list of taboos - unwritten rules that guide social behavior. Violating these can be seen as disrespectful, and Vietnam is no different. Here are some cultural taboos that you should be aware of:

- Respect Personal Space: Vietnamese people value personal space. Avoid touching others, especially on the head, as it's considered disrespectful.

- Mind Your Feet: In Vietnamese culture, the feet are considered the lowest part of the body. Never point your feet towards people or sacred items, such as statues of the Buddha.

- Dress Appropriately: When visiting religious sites or rural areas, dress modestly to respect the local customs.

- Mind Your Chopsticks: As previously mentioned, never stick your chopsticks upright in a bowl of rice, as it's reminiscent of incense sticks burning at a grave, symbolizing death.

- Avoid Public Displays of Affection: While times are changing, public displays of affection are generally frowned upon, especially in rural and conservative areas.

While this list is not exhaustive, it gives you a sense of the cultural sensitivity required when living in or visiting Vietnam. By being aware of these taboos and respecting local customs and traditions, you can avoid potential misunderstandings and ensure your interactions with locals are respectful and positive.

And there we have it! By understanding the critical laws, knowing what to avoid, and respecting the local culture, you're well-equipped to make your time in Vietnam not only enjoyable but also hassle-free and respectful of the Vietnamese way of life.

So, as you navigate through your time in Vietnam, remember to keep these legal and cultural pointers in mind, not just as rules to follow but as stepping stones to a deeper, more meaningful understanding of this vibrant and captivating country.

CONCLUSION

Well, dear reader, we've been through a lot together, haven't we? From the ins and outs of Vietnamese etiquette to the grand Vietnamese festivals, we've immersed ourselves in this vibrant culture. We've savored the flavors of Phở, navigated the bustling job market, and even learned how to avoid the wrath of a Vietnamese traffic cop!

Like a seasoned traveler, you've journeyed through the intriguing landscape of Vietnamese culture, picking up valuable insights, practical tips, and maybe even a few Vietnamese phrases along the way. And let's not forget the laughs we shared, the surprises we encountered, and the powerful connections we made with this incredible culture.

Now, as we conclude this enlightening journey, let's revisit some of the key takeaways from our adventure:

- Vietnamese culture is vibrant in history, tradition, and a unique way of life. Embracing it involves understanding its complexities, respecting its customs, and appreciating its beauty.

- Navigating the Vietnamese social and professional seas involves mastering the art of respect, harmony, and patience. Whether it's mastering the etiquette of a business meeting or winning the heart of a Vietnamese friend, every interaction is an opportunity to build bridges and foster meaningful connections.

- From bustling markets to tranquil temples, Vietnam's landscapes are as diverse as its people. Whether you're planning to work, marry, or simply explore Vietnam, this book has equipped you with the knowledge and tools to navigate these landscapes with confidence and ease.

But let's not forget that the journey of cultural adaptation isn't a one-time affair. It's a continuous dance, a perpetual learning curve.

So, what's the next step in your Vietnamese adventure? Well, that's up to you. Maybe you'll explore the fascinating world of Vietnamese art, immerse yourself in Vietnamese literature, or perhaps conquer the language mountain one phrase at a time.

No matter what your next steps are, remember to embrace the Vietnamese way - with respect, patience, and a hearty dose of enthusiasm. And as you continue your journey, remember to savor each moment, each experience, each connection. In the end, it's these moments that weave the vibrant tapestry of your Vietnamese adventure.

May your Vietnamese journey be as vibrant, enriching, and captivating as the culture itself! And remember, when it comes to exploring culture, there are no wrong steps, only new moves.

Good luck!

THOUGHTS & OPINIONS

Dear Readers,

I want to express my heartfelt appreciation for choosing to read my book. Your time and attention mean the world to me. If you enjoyed the journey through its pages, I kindly request your support in the form of a review.

Your honest feedback is invaluable, guiding potential readers and helping me grow as an author. Whether it's a few lines or a detailed account of your thoughts, your review will make a significant difference. Please take a moment to share your thoughts and impressions.

Thank you for being a part of my literary journey, and I look forward to hearing from you.

To leave a review, please visit your Amazon Order History and find "Understanding Vietnamese Culture and Etiquette" in your purchased items and choose "Write a Product Review" or scan the barcode below if you live in the US :

With gratitude,

Joyce T.

BOOK REFERENCES

Britannica. (2022). Vietnam. In Encyclopedia Britannica.

Commisceo Global. (2019). 3 Aspects of Vietnamese business culture you really need to know. In Commisceo Global.

Cultural Atlas. (2020). Vietnamese Culture - Family. In SBS Cultural Atlas.

Cultural Atlas. (2020). Vietnamese culture - Etiquette. In SBS Cultural Atlas.

EScholarship. (2002). Colonialism and communism in Vietnam. In EScholarship.

Global Etiquette. (2021). Cross-cultural marriage - Eight issues to consider before tying the knot. In Global Etiquette.

iTour Vietnam. (2017). Vietnamese gifts etiquettes. In iTour Vietnam.

iTour Vietnam. (2021). Vietnamese traditional gender roles. In iTour Vietnam.

IMF. (2020). Vietnam: Raising millions out of poverty. In IMF.

Ling App. (2022). Vietnamese tones. In Ling App.

Mondly. (2021). 120+ Core Vietnamese words and phrases for travelers. In Mondly.

Mondly. (2021). 120+ core Vietnamese words and phrases for travelers. In Mondly.

MSquare Media. (2022). 5 Key strategies for effective cross-cultural communication. In MSquare Media.

Nguyen, T. T. L. (2018). Language learning strategies among Vietnamese EFL high school students. In ResearchGate.

Packard Communications. (2021). Most common pronunciation errors for Vietnamese learners of English. In Packard Communications.

Statista. (2022). Vietnam - GDP distribution across economic sectors 2021. In Statista.

Study.com. (2022). How Chinese rule changed the Vietnamese. In Study.com.

The Knot. (2022). 13 traditions customarily seen in Vietnamese weddings. In The Knot.

TMF Group. (2023). Top challenges of doing business in Vietnam. In TMF Group.

Travel Sense Asia. (2020). Vietnamese dining etiquette – Best things to know. In Travel Sense Asia.

Unsplash. (n.d.). Beautiful free Images & Pictures Unsplash. Unsplash. https://unsplash.com/

Verbal Planet. (2022). How long does it take to learn Vietnamese? In Verbal Planet..

Vietnam Briefing. (2021). Business etiquette in Vietnam - Customs and tips. In Vietnam Briefing.

Vietnam Daily. (2019). Vietnamese tones. In Vietnam Daily.

Vietnam Drive. (2021). 8 Vietnamese traditional food that you may not miss. In Vietnam Drive.

Vietnam Online. (2022). Vietnam food culture: The basics. In Vietnam Online.

Vietnam Visa. (2021). The ultimate guide to customs and etiquette in Vietnam. In Vietnam Visa.

VietnamesePod101. (2022). Vietnamese vocabulary and phrases to use at a restaurant. In Vietnamese-Pod101.

Wikipedia. (2022). Women in Vietnam. In Wikipedia.

www.ingramcontent.com/pod-product-compliance
Lightning Source LLC
Chambersburg PA
CBHW020950160726
47994CB00006B/2152